Tony and Rhoda Lederer were for many years the best known and most successful bridge teaching partnership in England. Their informal, simple style, which made the game seem both entertaining and easy, was welcomed every year by hundreds of students.

This book recreates the early teaching under the Lederer methods in 'terms' of ten lessons each. It is intended for absolute beginners, taking them from the basics to the point where they need only experience to become reasonably sound players. The bidding methods followed are the simple ones: simple Acol with a weak No Trump and as few frills as possible presented in the conversational tone which made the Lederers' classroom style so successful. The book can be used by any beginner who may have been daunted by what he has learnt of the game elsewhere.

Learn Bridge with the Lederers

Tony and Rhoda Lederer

London
UNWIN PAPERBACKS
Boston   Sydney

First published in Great Britain by *Cassell Limited* 1977

First published by Unwin Paperbacks 1982
Second edition 1984
Third edition 1986

UNWIN® PAPERBACKS
40 Museum Street, London WC1A 1LU, UK

Unwin Paperbacks
Park Lane, Hemel Hempstead, Herts HP2 4TE, UK

George Allen & Unwin Australia Pty Ltd.,
8 Napier Street, North Sydney, NSW 2060, Australia

Unwin Paperbacks with the Port Nicholson Press
PO Box 11-838 Wellington, New Zealand

Copyright© Rhoda Lederer 1977, 1982, 1984, 1986

Graphics by Harry Palmer of Amersham

Lederer, Tony
    Learn bridge with the Lederers. — 3rd ed.
    1. Contract bridge
    I. Title   II. Lederer, Rhoda
    795.41'5   GV1282.3
    ISBN 0-04-793090-X

Typeset by Inforum Ltd, Portsmouth
Printed in Great Britain by
Hazell Watson & Viney Ltd,
Aylesbury, Bucks

Contents

Foreword

Ever since the English Bridge Union Teachers' Association was founded in 1971, Tony has been the Publications Officer, and his job has been to read all the new bridge books published far and wide, to see if they are suitable for recommendation to teachers or students of the game. However good a book may be, it is useless to suggest it if beginners would merely find it mystifying or if it expounds methods used only in Shangri-La. One of his most frequent comments has always been that the writers never seem to stress how simple the game of Contract Bridge is. 'You see how simple it is,' we say every time we demonstrate something on the blackboard, and often this becomes a catch-phrase chanted by the class even before we say it.

Please get it into your heads — it *is* a simple game. The only troublesome part about it is that there is so much you need to know before you can begin to play it. At the start of a bridge cruise, for example, we often hear students complaining that they are in a complete fog, and wondering why they ever set out to try to learn something so much beyond them. They go to bed bewitched, bothered and bewildered, but believe us, by elevenses in the morning, dawn is beginning to break, and by the end of the cruise they are playing away as though born to it.

Many people start reading a bridge book and find it so dull and difficult that they give up after a few pages. Please try to stick with this one. Bridge is simpler to understand than the complicated rules and regulations of the games you have unwisely given your grandchildren for Christmas and which, in the end, you probably find them explaining to you!

In the coming lessons we shall deal with all aspects of the game — at least with all you need to know to go out and enjoy yourselves with your friends or at the local club. There will be plenty more you can learn with years of experience, but you don't need to become expert enough to aspire to the Centre Court at Wimbledon to have a world of fun playing tennis, and the same applies to playing Contract Bridge.

Any of you who have already attended one of our courses may well think you can almost hear either Tony or Rhoda speaking, and so you may. We both have our favourite lessons, so when one is lecturing, the other sits at the side of the room and passes caustic comments. One student once said to us, 'How rude you are to each other!' This was at the start of the course, and at the end she said, 'I see just why you do it — anything that will help to make it stick in one's head is a help.' Well, that's the answer, isn't it? We shall try to give you our gimmicks and anything that will help you to remember, because all you need to learn is a good solid foundation, both of bidding and play.

What we have tried to do is to set out in a simple but progressive way, the 'lesson for the day'. Students on the whole tend to take massive, often incorrect and indecipherable notes, and some time later, when the point crops up again, you see them scrabbling frantically through their notebooks, and either failing to find the point, or discovering that they've got it wrong. Here the salient rules, which should be learned by heart, are set out clearly and simply in little boxes. They can be picked up very easily. Nor shall we tell you to do something without explaining why, because half the difficulty vanishes if you understand why you should do this or that.

Though this book is primarily intended as a class text book and a substitute for inaccurate notes, the actual tutors have not been forgotten. At the end of the book tutors will find some notes which, from our years of experience, we hope will help them. We hope this will help both tutors and students, and we also hope that this will relieve many of the dim foggy muddles so many students can get themselves into, sometimes — dare we say it? — almost because of their tutors rather than in spite of them.

So now let's get on with learning the game of Contract Bridge, now past its fiftieth birthday and gaining in popularity every day.

TONY and RHODA LEDERER

Since this foreword was written, as well as the notes for the various lessons and many of the lessons themselves, my very dear husband has died. He both inspired and wrote the bulk of the book but I have had to finish it, as I know he would have wanted me to do, without his incomparable help and inspiration. I have tried to keep it as I think he would have wished, a dual effort from both of us, and if even a few students come out the better players for it, I shall feel that I have succeeded in my task.

RHODA LEDERER
1977

1 What Contract Bridge is all about

The objects of the game — determining partnerships — cutting and shuffling — the auction — ranking of suits — the contract — value of points scored — scoring — a score card — vulnerability — hand valuation — Milton Work Count — 'length' points

---

Contract Bridge is a fascinating game, an enormous social asset, and a source of innumerable hours of enjoyment. You will even enjoy the process of learning, so let's get on with it as quickly as possible.

We shall assume that all of you have played some form of card game, so know the difference between the four suits and what is meant by winning a trick. However, in case anyone is completely ignorant, we'll start at the very beginning.

The object of the game is to win the Rubber. This is rather like winning a match in the Ladies' Doubles at Wimbledon — the best of three games. We said doubles deliberately because bridge is a game for four players but, unlike tennis, the two partnerships each face each other across the table.

Normally partnerships are determined by 'cutting', the two players drawing the two highest cards playing against the two with the two lowest cards. To organise 'the cut', take one of the two packs you will be using and spread it face down on the table. Each of the four who are to play draws a card, but *not* one of the four at either end of the spread pack – or next to a card drawn by any other player.

Who is to play with whom depends on knowing the ranking order of the four suits — remember this, as it's very important.

♠ = spades   ♡ = hearts
♢ = diamonds   ♣ = clubs

There are two simple ways of reminding yourselves, either the little mnemonic SHaDoC, or the fact that the suits rank in alphabetical order *upwards*. Each suit contains thirteen cards headed by the ace downwards — no jokers, please! — and the ace, king, queen, knave and ten are the 'honours'.

To take just two examples of how to determine the partnerships, suppose the four cut cards are the ♡Q, the ♠7, the ◇K and the ◇6. The two highest cards would be the ◇K and ♡Q, and the two lowest the ♠7 and ◇6. But what if the cut contained two, or even more cards of the same value? Say the ♡Q, the ♠7, the ◇7 and the ♣3. As spades rank higher than diamonds, the player with the ♠7 would play with the one who cut the ♡Q, leaving the ◇7 and ♣3 as the other partnership.

The player who cuts the highest card has all the advantages. He may choose where he will sit — with his partner facing him — and which of the two packs shall 'belong' to his side for the Rubber, the choice generally being between a red and a blue pack, and — don't ask us why — it is usually considered lucky to select the pack with which you won the cut. The highest cutter will become the first dealer, and the pack he has chosen will be shuffled, or thoroughly mixed, by the opponent on his left. It is then passed across to the opponent on the dealer's right who cuts the pack *once,* towards the dealer. The dealer closes the cut and deals the cards out, one at a time, until each player has thirteen cards. Meanwhile the dealer's partner will have been shuffling the second pack, and will place it on his right:

> 'If you're not demented quite,
> Place the cards upon your right.'

Now we come to a big difference from the game of Whist, which most of you probably know. In Whist the trump suit for each hand is pre-determined. The trump suit is the one with all the teeth, which will bite off the heads of the opposition's winners. In Contract Bridge we have an auction which, like any self-respecting auction, means that the players bid in turn (dealer first) and that each bid must out-rank the bid before it. Here we add another denomination to the four already named, and that is No Trumps, which ranks at the head of the list. It means as it sounds — you play the hand with no trump suit. Thus a player who 'opens the bidding' with, say, 1♡, can be out-ranked by a bid of 1♠ or 1NT, but it would require 2♣ or 2◇ to out-rank 1♡.

The auction continues clockwise round the table until three

players in rotation have said 'No Bid', which means they have nothing further to add to the auction. The final bid becomes the denomination in which the hand will be played, but the first player to name that denomination becomes 'declarer'. Here an example auction is needed, so accustom yourselves right from the start to thinking of the four players at the table as North, South, East and West, North and South being partners against East and West.

Apart from making cheerful noises about the suit you would prefer as trumps, you will also have been trying to discover which will suit you and your partner best. Solo players read, mark, learn and inwardly digest this, because in Contract Bridge you have a partner and are not out on your own as you are in Solo. Now here's our sample auction. North, the dealer on this hand,

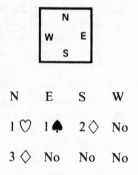

N	E	S	W
1♡	1♠	2♢	No
3♢	No	No	No

'opened' with 1♡, East 'intervened' with 1♠ and South 'responded' with 2♢. West had nothing to say ('No Bid') and North, liking South's suggestion of diamonds as trumps, 'raised' to 3♢, after which came three passes, or no bids. Note that although North was the last to bid, South was the first to make a bid in diamonds, so becomes 'declarer' for this hand. The player on declarer's left makes the opening lead, by taking a card from his hand and placing it on the table, and now declarer's partner puts his hand face up on the table, arranged neatly in suits with the trump suit, if any, on his right. From this point onwards we have a contract, a declarer, two defenders, and a dummy, who is declarer's partner.

The first six tricks won by declarer don't count towards his contract, in this case 3♢. The reason for this is that with 52 cards in the pack, there are 13 tricks available. If everything were absolutely evenly divided, each side would win 6½ tricks, but with four cards to a trick this is impossible, so if one side has 6 tricks, the other must have 7. In this instance to fulfil his contract, declarer must make 9 tricks, 6 + 3, with diamonds as trumps.

Remember we said earlier that the object of the game was to win the Rubber, the best of three games, so now you need to learn about scoring, as you want to try to sweep in and win your two games before your opponents frustrate you. The essence of the name 'Contract Bridge' is that you score towards your game only what you contract to make. Learn the following little table by heart:

Game = 100 points.   Rubber = the best of 3 Games

3 NT = 3 + the original 6 = 9, counting 40 for the first trick and 30 for each subsequent trick = 100 points.

4♡ or 4♠, 10 tricks in the 'major' suits, give game, as each trick over the first 6 = 30 points = 120 points.

5♣ or 5◇, 11 tricks in the 'minor' suits, give game, as each trick over the first 6 = 20 points = 100 points.

The necessary game score of 100 points can also be reached in gradual stages through two or more 'part-scores' adding up to 100, but the obvious danger here is that as soon as one side becomes *vulnerable* by bidding and making a game, a line is drawn across the score card, the opponents losing any part-score they may have towards their game, though all points scored by either side count in the final reckoning. Extra tricks, or 'over-tricks', for example 10 tricks made if you are in a 3-level contract requiring only 9 tricks, are scored 'above the line'. The full scoring table is given on p.197 but don't be scared of this, and don't even bother about it until you are much further on with your lessons — your tutor will explain the meaning of such mysteries as doubling, redoubling, and bonus points when you come to need them.

The first pair to win two games wins the Rubber. If it is a 3-game rubber the winners get 500 bonus points. If one pair has two games and the other none, the winners take 700 bonus points.

The declarer's object is to win at least the number of tricks he promised during the auction, and the defenders' is to prevent this. You and your partner are always 'We' on the score card and your opponents are 'They'. Everything scored on the way to game is scored below the horizontal line and everything else above it.

WE	THEY

Each time one pair wins a game, that is, 100 points below the line, a line is drawn across the card and both pairs start again from scratch. As already mentioned, a pair winning a game becomes *vulnerable* which means that all penalties incurred for failing to fulfil a contract are doubled. So once you are vulnerable you can't splash out too much, or risk bidding too high in an attempt to win a game or keep the other pair out.

Another important point is that each player in turn plays a card to the one led, and if you have a card of the suit led you *must* play it. The highest card of that suit wins the trick, and the player who played it leads to the next trick. If you haven't got a card of the suit led you may, if you wish, play a trump, which will take precedence over any other card already played and could only be beaten by a higher trump. For example, playing with hearts as trumps, the leader plays the ♠5, next hand the ♠10, third player the ♠A and fourth player the ♠8. The ♠A would win the trick and that player would lead first to the next trick. If, however, after the ♠5 and ♠10, the third player had no spade, he could play a trump, and even the lowly ♡2 would win the trick unless capped by a higher trump from the fourth player. Failure to 'follow suit' if you have a card of the suit led is known as a 'revoke', for which uncomfortable penalties can be incurred.

Now let's cut for partners, deal, bid and play. Bewitched, bothered and bewildered already? Don't worry, it will all come clean in the wash — in other words, with a little practice.

Hand Valuation: Let's start with the bidding, or language of bridge. You are not allowed to say to your partner that you have so many spades, hearts, diamonds or clubs, or so many aces, kings, and so on, but you've got to get these messages across to your partner and, equally important, understand his answers as well as any messages he sends you. Don't panic — you're not going to have to learn a completely new foreign language, and after your first few lessons you will find yourself using the language of bridge without difficulty.

Very rarely in this book shall we mention mathematics or odds as they scare people away, but we do use a simple point count which we want you to learn, as we shall be referring to it a lot in the following pages. Don't be dismayed — it's very simple, asking you to remember just five things:

Ace = 4 points: King = 3 points: Queen = 2 points: Knave = 1 point

In No Trump bidding only, 10 = a + value.

Thus the total 'honour' count in each suit is 10 points, and the total in the whole pack is 40 points. If all the high cards were evenly distributed, each player would find himself looking at 10 points, but life ain't like that, and almost always someone at the table will pick up more than his fair share. Assume you are the one with more than your share — say a modest 12 or 13 points. If the remaining 27 are evenly divided between the other three players, then your partner should have 9 points and your combined total would be 21 or 22 points. All things being equal, that is, allowing for no disasters, the magic number of points required to score a game in 3NT, 4♡ or 4♠ is 25-6. So 22 points is *not enough* to put you into the game range when you could draw your first line across the score-card, but it should be enough for at least a small part score. Your partner, however, could have a good deal more than his share of 9 points, or perhaps a good deal less. All this has to be discovered by the language of bidding. Very seldom will you have enough dynamite in your own hand to ignore your partner completely, so it is imperative that, as a pair, you should learn to exchange information, and to do it in such a way that you gain a complete picture of your two hands — in other words, you both know where you are going, and how high up the bidding mountain you can safely climb before you feel it necessary to stop.

Incidentally, it's worth mentioning at this point that you shouldn't sit there with eyes and ears closed if your opponents are bidding. There is much you may learn which can help you to produce an effective defence on the occasions when they win the contract, which, if things go fairly, should be about half the times.

Length Points: So much for the valuation of your hand by way of honour points, but there is one other thing to learn before you can take your first step and 'open the bidding'. If you decide your hand doesn't rate an opening bid, you say, 'No bid,' but if it looks reasonably picturesque you count it up, first the honour points by way of the Milton Work Count and then the additional bonus or 'length' points, if you have any. As prospective opener, you should add one point for every card over four in the suit you propose to suggest as trumps. There is a very good reason for this, which you may as well learn now as later. It is that you can always use a trump on a 'short' suit to stop the opposition making a lot of tricks in it, so the more trumps you have, the happier you will be. Using up a trump to win a trick when you started with only four *can* at times be an embarrassment, as it can reduce you to less trumps than your opponents have. But if you have five, or perhaps even six trumps, you won't mind using one, or even two, to trump enemy high cards. Thus 'long' trumps have a definite value, and it would be mad not to count them as part of your assets.

```
♠ K 9 2        ♠ K 9 2
♡ A K 8 3  or  ♡ A K 8 5 3
♢ A 7 5        ♢ A 7 5
♣ 8 7 4        ♣ 8 7
```

Here are a couple of example hands. On the first you have 14 honour points, and on the second you have exactly the same 14 honour points *plus* one extra point for the fifth heart. Both hands, therefore, taking 12 or 13 points as a minimum for an opening bid, are worth opening on — telling your partner you have the values to make a bid. What we should bid, and why, we shall learn in the following lessons.

2 Playing a hand in No Trumps

Knocking out opponents' entries — counting sure winners and making a plan — 'establishing' a suit — finessing

We know from experience that all the students really want to do is to get the cards in their hands and play. We also know that many people find it difficult to learn from a blackboard lecture, and that practical experience works wonders. For your first lesson, then, we are going to show you the simplest of the basic facts about playing a hand in No Trumps. Don't worry about the bidding, as you will come to that in the next lesson.

Knocking Out Opponents' Entries: One of the very hardest things for a learner to do is deliberately to lose a trick. They love to 'cash' all their lovely top winners and then sit back and wonder what has happened when a wheel comes off and the contract fails. Let's suppose you are South on the hand shown overleaf, playing in 6 NT, which means you must make twelve tricks. West, on lead, plays the ◇Q and you take your first step which is to count your certain tricks. You have four top spades, three top hearts and two top diamonds, one of which you are going to use on the first trick. If you happily 'cash' all these, you will have nine tricks only, and all you will have left is the ♣K-Q-J-10. You will have to play one of them, and if West wins with the ♣A, he will reel off all the rest of his diamonds, leaving you three down on your contract.

What would have happened, however, if after winning the first trick, and *whilst you still have a winning diamond,* you coura-

♠ A Q 7
♡ 9 6 4 2
♢ 8 5 4
♣ 7 6 3

♠ K J 8 5
♡ A K Q
♢ A K
♣ K Q J 10

geously lead the ♣ K? We know it's a loser, but if West wins the trick you forestall any hope he has of playing off his diamonds. He can lead another of the suit, but *you* will win, and you will have 'established' three club tricks for yourself. If you add these to your other certain winners, you will find the total is twelve tricks, or 6NT bid and made.

Go back over the hand above and look at it with the East and West hands as they well may be:

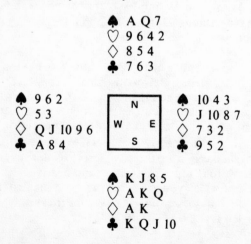

♠ A Q 7
♡ 9 6 4 2
♢ 8 5 4
♣ 7 6 3

♠ 9 6 2
♡ 5 3
♢ Q J 10 9 6
♣ A 8 4

♠ 10 4 3
♡ J 10 8 7
♢ 7 3 2
♣ 9 5 2

♠ K J 8 5
♡ A K Q
♢ A K
♣ K Q J 10

If you cash all your winners, East will 'discard' everything but his ♣ A and his diamonds and then, because you have nothing else to play, you lead a club, and you can't prevent him from winning and himself 'cashing' the diamonds you will have established for him. How different it is if, having been attacked in diamonds, you hang on like glue to your second stop in the suit and knock out his ♣A whilst you still have stops in the other suits as well. In other words, you must be sure to go for the clubs at the second trick. Never mind losing a trick — we know it hurts beginners, but you will find that time and time again it is vital to success.

The important lesson to learn here is twofold — try to knock out the enemy 'entries' whilst you still have control of their suit, and don't release the 'guards' you may hold in their suit until you have done this.

Counting your certain winners and deciding where your tricks are to come from is of primary importance. Remember that your opponents will almost certainly have attacked by leading their longest and strongest suit, so that any 'stops' which will prevent them from running off winners in it are of vital importance.

Life isn't always quite as easy as we have made this hand, and sometimes you will have to choose carefully which suit you will try to 'establish' for your contract.

        ♠ A Q 8
        ♡ A K
        ◇ Q J 9 7
        ♣ K J 6 2

        N
    W   E
        S

        ♠ K 9 3
        ♡ 7 4
        ◇ K 10 8 6 2
        ♣ Q 10 9

Again you are South, declarer in 3NT against which West leads a heart. You immediately count your winners — three spades, two hearts, four diamonds once the ace has been knocked out, and three clubs once that ace has been knocked out. Which suit do you go for first, whilst you still have a heart guard? Clearly the diamonds will yield four tricks for certain, so that you can take your nine tricks before the rats get at them. Your second top heart will go when you start on the diamonds, but that won't matter. What *will* matter is if you start on the clubs, because you can only make three tricks in the suit and will *also* have to work on the diamonds, and the opposition has the ace of that suit too.

Now we'll change the hand and also put in a very probable distribution of the East and West hands. See if you can work out how you should plan the play of the hand before you even start on the first trick — and that means don't look at the East and West hands.

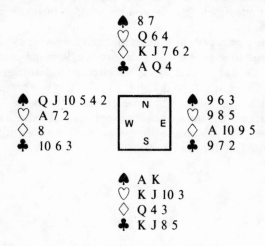

Remember you're in the driving seat so it's all up to you. West leads a spade — have you counted your tricks? Two spades and four clubs — not enough for your 3NT contract, so the rest must come from hearts and diamonds — or is it *or* diamonds? You have attractive length in diamonds, eight cards as compared with seven in hearts *but the diamonds might go wrong,* whereas in hearts nothing can go wrong once you've knocked out the ace. You have three certain heart tricks, but if the diamonds don't produce three tricks, you will have to lose to both red aces which you can't afford, as by then your second spade stop will have gone. So it is imperative to go for the hearts immediately, to make sure of your contract. Now look at the East-West hands and see the pit you would have dug for yourself if you'd touched the diamonds.

Finessing: There are various other important techniques of card play which you will have to learn before you can really play a hand, but at this stage we only propose to teach you the important art of 'finessing', which really boils down to giving yourself the chance to make a trick out of thin air.

◇ A Q 8

◇ 6 5 4

Look at this little diagram. Again you are in the driving seat and, naturally, want to make as many tricks as you can. In fact you can't see how to fulfil your contract if you don't make two diamond tricks. If you lead a diamond and play the ace and then lead another from dummy, you will make exactly one diamond trick, because whoever has the other high honours will step in smartly and win the other two. But half the times the ◇K will be in the West hand, and half the times it will be in the East hand. If it is with West, and you lead *from* your South hand and play the queen, it will win. If East has the king there's nothing you can do about it, but you have a half-and-half chance, so why not take it?

♣ K Q 8

♣ 6 5 4

Similarly here, if you want two club tricks you must cross your fingers and pray that West has the ♣A. If you play a high honour from dummy, *whoever* has the ace will win with it, you will make one top club, but the opposition will grab the third round with the knave. If West has the ♣ A and you lead *towards* the king, either West will play the ace if he has it, in which case both your king and queen will have become winners, or he will hold it up, in which case one of your two top honours will win. You don't now spoil everything by playing the second one, but wait till you can get back to your own hand and do it all over again. Look at a possible full distribution of the suit:

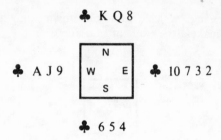

♣ K Q 8

♣ A J 9   ♣ 10 7 3 2

♣ 6 5 4

The only way to make two club tricks is for West to hold the ace. If East has it, that's just too bad, but if you're unlucky half the times, you'll be lucky the other half.

♡ 7 4

♡ K 8 3

So that you don't get the idea that it is always a matter of leading from the South hand towards dummy, here's another situation which is really a finesse. If you play a heart from your own South hand you won't win a heart trick, but if you play a heart from dummy *towards* your king, half the time you will find East has the ace, which he either plays or holds up, as the mood takes him, so that you will win a heart trick.

Golden Rule:
Lead *from* nothing (the hand with the little cards) *towards* something (the hand with the high cards)

Sometimes you can make life easier for yourself if just one high card is missing and your own high cards are split between your hand and dummy. In our next diagram the king is missing, and if West has it you needn't lose a spade trick. Nor will you have to organize entries because you can do it all in one. The queen, knave, ten and nine are all the same value as they run in sequence. Lead the queen from your own hand and if West doesn't 'cover an honour with an honour' (which you will learn about in due course) 'run' the queen, that is, play the six from dummy. If West

♠ A 10 9 6

♠ Q J 7

has the king your queen will win the trick and you can repeat the
agony for him by next leading the knave. If he still doesn't cover,
you have the spade seven left to lead towards dummy's remaining
ace and ten, so that even if West started with four spades to the
King, *you* will win all four spade tricks.

◇ A Q 10 9

◇ 5 4 2

In the next example you will see that you are missing both the
king and the knave. Play low from your own South hand and, if
West also plays small, play North's nine. If West happens to hold
both the king and knave, your nine will win the trick and you will
organise a return to your own hand to repeat the finesse. If East
wins with the knave you still don't know where the king is, but you
have nothing to lose by trying the finesse again later. Obviously if
East wins the first trick with the king, you *know* that West has the
knave, because East wouldn't have wasted the king unless he had
had to, so next time you're in your own hand, play a second low
diamond and put on the ten, fully confident that it will win.

Lastly, let's suppose you have something like this combination:

♡ Q 6 4

♡ A 5 2

Time and again we have seen beginners crossing carefully to dummy and leading the queen, and when questioned as to why, they have said they are finessing for the king. What actual good can this possibly have done? If East has the ♡ K he will learn that he must, in a position such as this, cover an honour with an honour, so he will put on the king and you will have to play the ace to win the trick, leaving yourself with only two small cards in the suit in either hand. If West has the king and you 'run' the queen by playing low from the South hand, he will slap it smartly on your queen, and once again you will win only one heart trick. Your only hope, until very much later in your studies, when you learn more advanced techniques, is to do that finger-crossing job whilst praying that West has the ♡ K. If you lead low from the South hand towards your queen, either West will play low and your queen will win the trick, or he will put up the king, in which case your queen will live to fight another day.

You may think this contradicts our golden rule about leading from nothing towards something but it doesn't really, because almost certainly, just in case East or West had the bare king — that is, a singleton — you would have cashed the ace first, reducing the South holding to nothing.

Put the ♡ J in the North hand instead of the six and give yourself the ten instead of the five, and now if East has the king, by leading the queen you will not lose a heart trick, whereas if you lead from your big something, the ace, towards your lesser something, you will lose a trick to the king whoever has it.

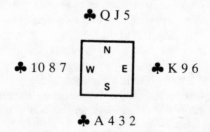

♣ Q J 5

♣ 10 8 7   W E   ♣ K 9 6

♣ A 4 3 2

Even with a holding like this, don't lead the ♣ Q or, when East covers, you will 'promote' West's ♣ 10. Your best bet is to lead low from South towards the ♣ Q J 5, and if West has the ♣ K you will make three club tricks.

3 Weak No Trump opening bids and responses

A limit bid — typical 'shape' — combined points required — direct 'quantitative' No Trump raises — the weak take-out — the jump take-out — jump direct to game — bidding to game or part-score

From a teacher's point of view it doesn't really matter whether your first real lesson on bidding deals with No Trumps or suit openings, but we consider No Trumps so important that we are taking this subject first. Don't worry at the lesson heading, if you have heard of a strong No Trump — we shall teach you that all in good time but to start with let's take what is one of the most potent weapons in bridge, the weak No Trump.

There are various reasons why it is so potent. Firstly, as you have already learned, every bid in the auction must go at least one step higher than the one before it, and as No Trumps tops the ranking order, no opponent can join in below the two-level, which may be very difficult and dangerous for him. Secondly you will find that you pick up in the region of twelve or thirteen points, very near your natural share of ten, time and time again, and using a weak No Trump you can get into the action very early, causing the maximum obstruction to the enemy. If you use a strong No Trump you may wait all afternoon — or evening — for the necessary points, which are far more than your natural share, and you will have to depend on some form of 'prepared' opening (see Lesson 20) if you are to speak at all on the weaker hands.

Limit Bid: An opening bid of 1NT is a *limit bid*. Whatever its strength, which you must, of course, agree with your partner and announce to the opposition, you must keep within the agreed limits. These should be within a spread of three points, and for the purposes of this lesson we suggest that you should keep to 12-14 points in an evenly balanced hand. By evenly balanced, we mean with a distribution of 4-3-3-3 or perhaps 4-4-3-2 in each of the suits. Ideally you will have a 'guard', that is a card likely to win a trick, in each of the four suits, but you can't have all this and heaven too. Contract bridge is a battle between two sides, and if you are to deploy your forces to the best effect you must use strategy, and not always think only of safety first.

Remembering your point count, which was set out on p.6, have a look at a few typical examples of a weak No Trump opening:

a) ♠ K 7 4	b) ♠ Q 9 6 2	c) ♠ A J 7
♡ Q 9 2	♡ 10 3	♡ K 9 2
◇ K 8 5	◇ A K 7 6	◇ A 9 8 4
♣ A J 6 5	♣ K 7 5	♣ 9 8 6

All three hands fall into the limit of 12-14 points, and none of them has an outstanding suit which you wish to tell your partner would be suitable as trumps. Hand (a) has the merit of having 'something in everything', (b) is short in hearts but, as you will see later, we have plenty of machinery for getting over that sort of difficulty, and (c) is completely evenly balanced, even if it hasn't got a guard, or stop, in clubs. Get into the action as quickly as you can, by opening 1NT.

As this is a *limit bid* you have already accomplished something — you have told your partner that you have not less than 12 points and not more than 14. Now learn another little table, and you will begin to see how simple this game really is:

Points required to make game or slam:
 9 tricks for game in No Trumps requires 25-6 points
10 tricks for game in ♠ or ♡ (major suits) requires 26 points
11 tricks for game in ◇ or ♣ (minor suits) requires 28-9 points
12 tricks for 'little slam' in a suit contract requires 31-3 points
12 tricks for 'little slam' in No Trumps requires 33-4 points
13 tricks for 'grand slam' in a suit or No Trumps requires 37 points

Don't bother about 'slams' for the moment. They will come later, but are in the table because you can get superb bonus points for bidding right up to a six or seven contract. Just now let's concentrate on that 25-6 points required for a game in No Trumps. Already your partner knows that you have 12-14 points in an evenly balanced hand. If he too has an evenly balanced hand suitable for play in No Trumps, how simple it is for him to judge what to 'respond'.

No Trump Raises: If your partner has 10 or less points, he can mentally add these to your known maximum of 14, and he *knows* that between you, you haven't got enough for game, so he just says, 'No bid.' If he has 11-12 points, his mental addition reveals that if you have your maximum of 14 points you have enough for game, but that if you have your minimum of 12 points, you haven't. So now he makes an *invitational* raise to 2NT. You can pass this if you are minimum or yourself go on to 3NT if you are maximum.

Lastly, if your partner himself knows that your combined values must come up to the required point-count, he won't put the weight on you by making an invitational raise, but will bid 3NT direct.

Later on you will come to other bigger raises designed to try to reach the mighty heights of a slam, but forget about these for now.

The Weak Take-Out: Often the responding hand, knowing that opener has 12-14 points in an evenly balanced hand, will obviously be unsuitable for play in No Trumps. Could anything be more horrible than a hand like this for a partner struggling to make seven tricks in No Trumps — because you won't, of course, even have considered making a No Trump raise on only 2 points?

$$\spadesuit \;\; 10\;9\;8\;6\;4\;2$$
$$\heartsuit \;\; Q\;6\;3$$
$$\diamondsuit \;\; 8\;4$$
$$\clubsuit \;\; 9\;3$$

Your spades, however, *must* be of use if they are trumps. Partner can't have bid his No Trump with less than two spades, so you will have at least eight trumps, which you will shortly learn is the magic number to give control of the suit, between the two hands. Bid 2♠. This suit bid at the lowest available level is a *weak take-out*. It categorically denies the values to go to game or the holding of a No Trump type of hand, and warns partner to bid no more.

You can make a weak take-out into spades, hearts or diamonds. Notice that we are not mentioning a take-out into 2 ♣ at the moment, as this has a special meaning which we shall come to in a later lesson.

If you don't fancy your responding hand for a No Trump contract but have only a 5-card suit it is, perhaps, more difficult to judge what action to take, and you may well never know until you see partner's hand go down on the table. Let's look at a couple of examples:

(a) ♠ 8
    ♡ 10 9 7
    ◇ A K 9 5 3
    ♣ 9 7 6 4

(b) ♠ Q 8
    ♡ J 9 7 5 4
    ◇ 9 3
    ♣ Q 10 7 6

You have no hope of making a game facing 12-14 points with hand (a), but it is not attractive, with nothing at all in three suits, for play in No Trumps, so make a weak take-out into 2◇. On hand (b), however, you can't really guess whether you can play more safely in hearts or No Trumps, so probably it is wiser, since you can't count game values, to pass.

Let's get one thing very clear at this point. No Trump bidding is a matter of simple arithmetic. Both partners know the agreed strength of the opening No Trump bid, and in responding to 1NT it is only necessary to decide whether you have the combined values for a game or not. If you haven't, then you either pass, make the invitational raise in No Trumps mentioned on p. 19, or make a weak take-out because you have decided that the hand will play better in your suit than in No Trumps. It doesn't matter what strength of No Trump you are using as responder merely gears his bids to the known strength — or weakness — facing him. What may be only a weak take-out hand facing a weak No Trump may be worth a game raise facing a strong No Trump.

The Jump Take-Out in Major Suits: If a simple bid at the lowest available level, that is two, is a weak take-out and a warning to partner to shut up, it goes without saying that you must have a means of alerting him to the fact that you have the values for game but that, for your money, you would prefer to play in a suit. This you do by making a *jump bid*, 1 NT-3♡, for example. Now you have said to partner that, knowing the values he holds, you want to play in a game contract, but that you would prefer to play in hearts. Look at these two hands:

♠ K J 8 7 6 3	♠ A K J 7 6 3
♡ A 8	♡ A 8
◇ 10 9 6	◇ 10 9 6
♣ 8 5	♣ 8 5

Facing 12-14 points this first hand is worth no more than a weak take-out into 2♠, an obviously wiser contract than 1NT. The second hand, however, with 12 honour points and a 6-card suit, is clearly worth a game contract, and you tell your partner this, at the same time announcing your good spade suit, by bidding 3♠. This is what is known as *game forcing,* and partner is not allowed to pass. He must either rebid 3NT, which he will do if your jump suit bid has struck a doubleton in his hand, or he will support spades with three or more of the suit.

This last sentence is very important, because you could well want to make a jump bid in a suit of only 5-card length. We've already mentioned that a combined eight cards in the trump suit is the ideal minimum to give you control. Suppose your hand is something like this:

| ♠ 9 |
| ♡ A Q J 9 8 |
| ◇ K Q 7 4 |
| ♣ Q 8 6 |

You certainly have the values for game, but your spade singleton makes you a little wary of playing in No Trumps. On the other hand, if partner has only two hearts you will have a total of seven, not really comfortable. Respond 3♡ and partner, who *must* bid again, will tell you if he has no better than a doubleton by rebidding 3NT or, with three or four hearts, will raise you to 4♡. Incidentally, the fewer hearts he has, the more likely he is to have spades, so there's no need to panic if you get a rebid of 3NT. In the previous hand, where you had a 6-card suit, there is nothing to stop you from removing a 3NT rebid into 4♠ if you want to do so.

We deal with the minor suits (◇ and ♣) differently, but don't worry about this yet.

Jump Take-Out to Game Level: You may well ask why, if you are permitted to remove 3NT to four of your suit, you don't bid direct to game in the first place. This is because a double jump take-out, 1NT-4♡, for example, has a special meaning. It shows a highly distributional hand with which you don't care if partner has only a doubleton of your suit and which, because of its 'shape', you are convinced is worth a try for game.

♠ A Q 10 9 7 6 4
♡ 8
◇ J 8 6 3
♣ 5

Here, for instance, your only interest is to play in spades, and you have every hope of making a game, so bid 4♠ direct.

There are lots more twiddly bits you will learn later, but you mustn't try to run before you can walk. There are, for example, special bids which mean something other than what you might expect. You won't meet the first of these until Lesson 10 and for the time being we shall keep everything basic and simple. Once you've got a good strong foundation of fact into your heads, you can learn to elaborate a bit. One thing always to remember is that an opening bid facing an opening bid is worth a game contract. Don't put the weight on partner by leaving him to guess, but make sure he gets there.

Finally, you may notice that we have spoken of nothing but bidding to game. It is very important to learn to do this because it means you will be learning to value your hand to the full. At Rubber Bridge, however, you may well have a part-score below the line, let's say 60 points. Now you only need 40 points to make up your 100 for a game. If partner opens 1NT there is no need to raise him as he's already bid enough for game, so on a modest hand just pass. If your part-score is 40 points, you need 60 to make up the game. With 13-14 points, needing a full game, you would raise 1NT direct to 3NT. Now, with no ambitions to go further for a slam, you would simply bid 2NT which completes the contract needed for game, and is no longer the invitational bid we explained on p. 19.

Throughout your lessons on bidding we shall always teach you to bid up to a game if this is possible, but don't forget that at Rubber Bridge this part-score aspect will always come into it.

Responding to an opening 1NT (12-14 points)
Pass on less than 11 points as 10 + 14 can't make up 25-6
Raise *invitationally* to 2NT on 11-12 points, as if opener has 14 rather than 12 points, you have enough for game.
Raise direct to 3NT on 13+ points as you have enough for game anyway.

4 Suit Opening Bids and Limit Bid Responses

Hands not suitable for a No Trump contract — to trump, or 'ruff' — 'long' trumps — a biddable suit — limit bid responses — responder's hand valuation — first mention of change-of-suit responses — responding to a minor-suit opening

Having dealt with evenly balanced hands on which you have no particular suit you would like to suggest as trumps, let's now turn to the hands on which you have a preference for a suit contract, or even perhaps a choice of two suits, when you want to try to discover which one your partner prefers.

We have put high walls around the ranges of strength required for bids and responses, because at no stage of your life as a bridge player should you make things difficult for yourself or your partner. Give messages, receive messages, and don't get into a position where either of you is out on a limb and doesn't know what to do. Never do you want headaches — leave this to the experts who, believe us, create plenty for themselves.

Now then, let's get on with hands on which you will open the bidding with a suit. We'll take it gradually so that you don't get confused and remember too that bidding a suit doesn't necessarily mean you won't end up playing in No Trumps. The language of bidding is designed to find out what contract is most suitable for you *and* your partner. Look first at this hand:

♠ A Q 8
♡ A J 10 8
◇ K 7 6
♣ A 9 2

We've already learned that evenly balanced hands containing 12-14 points are best opened 1 NT. Now why can't you open 1 NT on this hand? It couldn't be more evenly balanced so there must be a reason, and the reason is that you must never tell a lie. If you bid 1 NT you promise partner that you've got no *less* than 12 points and no *more* than 14. Not true, because you've got 18. So what do you do? You open one of your longest suit and, as you will learn in a later lesson, express your extra strength by your rebid.

    ♠ A Q 8
    ♡ A J 10 8 7
    ♢ K 7 6
    ♣ 9 8

Now let's take a hand which is not evenly balanced. As you will remember from Lesson 1, you should add one point for each card more than four in the suit you wish to suggest as trumps. Clearly your short clubs could prove an embarrassment in No Trumps whereas, if you play the hand in hearts, you can trump the third round if the opposition attacks you in that suit. To trump means, of course, that once you have no club with which to follow suit, you can use a trump to win the trick. Here you must learn a new word: to use a trump, or trump an opponent's card, is called 'to ruff'. Remember this, as from now on we shall use this correct bridge term. It may help you to remember if we tell you the true story of our non-bridge-playing secretary who was typing an article from dictation, and she ruffled a club on the table! We always picture that poor little club lying there ruffled and tatty. 'On the table,' by the way, means in dummy's hand, the one which is spread for declarer to play as well as his own.

Going back to the hand itself, you have 14 high-card or honour points plus one for the fifth heart, so you have a 15-point hand. Take away one of the clubs and make it into a sixth heart, and you would have a 16-point hand.

The reason why you can add this value to 'long' trumps is because they protect you from attack in a suit in which you have little or nothing. With our particular example, if the opposition leads off with the three top clubs, at least you can't lose more than the first two, as you can spare a trump for the third. This you could well not afford with only four trumps, as it could reduce you to a point where you had fewer trumps than your opponents.

To open the bidding in a suit you should set your sights on a minimum of 13 points, counting length points as well as high cards. As your experience grows you may well reduce this, but for the moment you want some values to play with.

We have already mentioned that the magic number of trumps between your hand and your partner's is eight. Disasters do sometimes occur when the 'distribution' of the adverse trumps is bad, but generally four trumps in each hand, or five in one and three in the other, makes life comfortable for declarer.

If you've now got the idea of how to choose your opening bid we can go a stage further, though some of you may already be wondering how to open if you pick up a veritable picture gallery or a tremendous long suit. Don't worry — we'll get to that all in good time, but for now we are considering only hands suitable for a one-level opening bid. These will normally contain between 13 and 19 points.

A 4-card suit is always biddable, but is not rebiddable, though as learners you would be well advised to have at least one high honour at the head of your suit. This is not always possible, as you will see if you look at the next example:

♠ 9 7 6 2
♡ A K Q
♢ A Q 5
♣ K 7 2

Here you can't open 1 NT as you have far too many points. Many players would choose to open what is called a 'prepared' 1♣, but please resist the temptation to fall into these evil ways. If you work on the knowledge that, if you open 1♠, partner will know that you may only have four of them, and won't 'raise' you in spades without himself holding four, you will find you come to no harm.

Limit Bid Responses: We treat the major and minor suits somewhat differently so first let's deal with the major suits, hearts and spades. Ten tricks are enough to score you a game, whereas in the minor suits, clubs and diamonds, you need eleven tricks for a game, and who wants to climb all that way up to the stars if you can discover that you can settle for a nine-trick contract in No Trumps?

Dealing strictly with hearts and spades, then, if you open one of either and partner 'raises' you, he is guaranteeing that he has four cards of your suit. Now you will know if you have the magic eight between you and have no need to look for any other spot to play the hand. Eight trumps should control any weaknesses, and even if partner's four turn out to be only small ones, the opposition's high honours will probably come crashing down on top of each other, leaving you and dummy as the only two at the table holding the cards with the teeth — the power to bite off the heads of the opposition's winners.

Here come the high walls we promised you at the start of this lesson. If partner's responding hand comes within the confines of a *limit bid,* that and no other is the correct bid. Its prime requisite is four of the trump suit, after which responder must go into a little huddle with himself as to the number of points he holds.

If opener bids 1♠ or 1♡ and responder has four or more cards in the suit:

  With 0-5 points, pass (say 'No Bid')
  With 6-9 points, raise 1♠ or 1♡ to 2♠ or 2♡
  With 10-12 points, raise 1♠ or 1♡ to 3♠ or 3♡
  With 13-15 points, raise 1♠ or 1♡ to 4♠ or 4♡

Do you see how simple this really is? Turn back to the table in Lesson 3, p. 18 and remind yourself of the number of points you need to score a game. If you open with one of a major suit and partner gives you a single raise, he is saying that he has four of your suit, not less than six points and not more than nine, and it shouldn't be very difficult for you to add his announced values to your own and decide whether you are in the part-score or game range. Similarly, if he gives you a double raise to the three-level he is promising you even better values, so you need a bit less yourself to take an optimistic view of a game contract. Remember, however, that a limit bid is *never forcing,* so you can always pass if you don't fancy the chances if you go on to game. But never be a coward — if partner raises you and you can see that your combined values are in the game zone, then bid the game.

If partner has 13-15 points, he will know that you are in the game zone and will see that you reach it. Later on we shall show you more scientific ways of dealing with these stronger responding hands, but for now stick to the little table. If responder has more than 15 points? Forget it until a later lesson.

As usual, we've now got to a point when there is something new to learn, and the first and all-important rule is that once a player has made a *limit bid,* a bid which expressly states his precise values within a narrow margin of points, the limit-bidder will not speak again unless his partner makes a bid which forces or encourages him to do so. This we shall come to later, but what it boils down to is that if the bidding goes 1♠-2♠-3♠, it's no good expecting the 2♠ bidder to pipe up again — he's said his little all and that's the end of his bidding life.

Responder's Hand Valuation: As opener you have learned to add one point for each card more than four in the prospective trump suit. Responder's valuation is a trifle different, but still very easy to learn. Provided he has four trumps, he adds points for 'shortages'.

Responder, with a minimum of 4-card trump support for opener, adds:

   3 points for a void (no card in a side-suit)
   2 points for a singleton (only one card in a side-suit)
   1 point for a doubleton (only two cards in a side-suit)

The terms are self-explanatory, but perhaps a word about the reason is needed. Once responder *knows* there is a minimum of eight trumps between the two hands, he also knows that his own four trumps will control weaknesses or shortages in side-suits (which are, of course, suits other than trumps). The quickest way to learn to understand these, and the other responses, will be from examples.

a) ♠ 9 8 6 4   b) ♠ J 9 6 4   c) ♠ J 9 8
      ♡ 8 7 5   ♡ 8 7 5   ♡ 8 7 5
      ◇ A Q 9 6 2   ◇ A K 9 8 2   ◇ A K 9 6 2
      ♣ 7   ♣ 7   ♣ 7 3

On hand (a), if partner opens 1♠, you can count six honour points and two for the singleton club, which makes eight and comes into the category of a single raise to 2♠ On hand (b) if partner opens 1♡, you 'change the suit' to 2◇, but if he opens 1♠ you have eight honour points plus two for the club singleton, so raise to 3♠. Note that on neither hand must you show the diamonds if partner has opened 1♠. Stick to the limit bid, showing the four-card trump support. On hand (c) you can't raise either spades or hearts, so must bid 2◇.

If, in the cases of hands (a) and (b), you make the mistake of bidding the diamonds when partner has opened 1♠, you will never be able to convince him that you have 4-card spade support. On hand (c) you can't raise either major suit, and will have to settle for 2◇ and await partner's rebid.

Responding to a Minor-Suit Opening: As we've already said, if your suit is a minor, you are really more interested in finding out if you can play in 3 NT than in a five-level contract, so responder may use the limit bids in exactly the same way, and using the same values, if there is no possibly more constructive bid to be made.

a) ♠ 9 7 4   b) ♠ K 9 7 5   c) ♠ K 9 7 5
   ♡ K 8 6   ♡ K 8 5   ♡ K 8 5
   ◇ Q 9 8 5   ◇ Q 9 8   ◇ Q 9 8 5
   ♣ K 7 4   ♣ K 7 5   ♣ K 7

On hand (a) if partner opens 1◇ you have no other bid to make than 2◇, expressing your 4-card diamond support and 6-9 point count. On hand (b) you can't raise diamonds, but speak you must. Bid 1♠, which may help partner into a No Trump contract. Compare, however, hand (c), which is where the crunch comes. If partner opens 1◇ you have the values to raise to 3◇, but is that going to get you far? All you will have said is that you have 10-12 points and four diamonds, and partner may well not dare to 'shoot' to either 5◇ or 3 NT. Tell him of your 4-card spade suit by bidding 1♠. After all, with 'something in everything', you will be quite happy if he merely rebids his diamonds or rebids in No Trumps. You won't get left out on a limb, because the change of suit forces opener to bid again.

Worrying about the future and where all this is getting you? Well, don't. We're going to switch off bidding for the next lesson, and show you how and why to play the cards when you have become declarer in a suit contract.

5 Suit Establishment and Trump Management

Whether to draw trumps or not — the ruff purposeless — ruffing in the 'short' hand — constructive reasons for drawing trumps — establishing a side-suit — unblocking

We've now come to the point when, because we fear a particular suit, and because we have discovered a mutual trump fit with partner, we've decided to play the hand with a trump suit rather than in No Trumps. The most important thing is to decide very early on in the hand whether you should draw trumps — extract the enemy teeth so that they can't wade in and 'ruff' (remember the word?) your winners, or whether you can put your trumps to better use first. This involves *thinking* before you start to play.

Here's another golden rule — the more quickly you grab a card from dummy as soon as the hand goes down, the worse player you prove yourself to be. Pause at Trick 1 and make your plan. The opposition may show signs of impatience and try to hurry you, but they'll laugh like silly if you oblige them and then, at about trick 8, find you've got yourself into a hopeless mess.

There is an old adage that more people are sleeping on the Embankment because they failed to draw trumps than for any other reason, but like most adages, this is open to question. Remember the pedestrians' Green Cross Code, which is stop, look both ways and listen before you leave the kerb — or play a card!

With plenty of trumps between the two hands you can generally afford to draw them, but suppose you've got a situation like this:

♠ 6 5 3
♡ 7

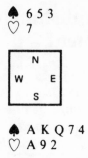

♠ A K Q 7 4
♡ A 9 2

Never mind about the rest of the hand — the plain fact of the matter is that with spades as trumps you have eight, which leaves five for the opposition, and they can't 'break' better than 3-2. If you draw three rounds you will have no trumps left in dummy. You have the ♡ A, but unless you can do something about it, which you won't be able to do if you have drawn all the trumps, you will have two losing hearts. On the other hand, if you can cash the ♡A, and then ruff a heart in dummy, then return to your own hand and ruff another heart *before* you draw trumps, you will have turned two losers into winners.

Now let's suppose you have an absolutely gorgeous trump suit such as ♡ A-K-Q-J-10-9. Here you have six certain tricks, and no amount of ruffing *dummy's* losers is going to turn them into more than six tricks. In fact to lead something from dummy and ruff it with a certain winner is doing no more than producing what that very famous duo Nico Gardener and Victor Mollo call the 'ruff purposeless'. The plain fact is that you can create extra tricks by ruffing in the 'short' hand (which means no more than the hand which has fewer trumps than the other), but you can't create extra tricks by ruffing with winners in the 'long' hand. This is true even if your suit isn't as gorgeous as the one above. Give yourself, perhaps, A-K-Q-4-3-2 facing three small ones. You have nine cards between you and dummy, and it is a mathematical fact that the four outstanding are more likely to break 3-1 than anything else. You almost certainly have six trump tricks, and if you cash your A-K-Q you will have none left in dummy, but if you've planned things carefully you may well be able to find a way of putting dummy's three to use.

Don't run away with the idea that you may never deliberately use a trump in the long hand. Of course you may, *if it serves some constructive purpose*. For learners there are four purposes:

1) To draw the opposition's teeth.
2) To get back from dummy to your own hand when no other convenient 'entry' is available.
3) To control a suit played by the opposition in which you are void.
4) To establish a suit in dummy on which you may later be able to discard your tram tickets. (Sorry! Tram tickets are worth their weight in gold as collectors' pieces nowadays, so let's say bus tickets.)

What we never want to see is a student climbing carefully over to dummy and leading a loser, only to ruff it with a winner in the long hand, when there is no purpose whatsoever in doing this.

The first three purposes set out above speak for themselves. Let's now look at this important business of 'establishing' a side-suit. First an example hand:

♠ Q 5 4
♡ 7
◇ A K 9 7 5 3
♣ 8 6 4

♠ A K J 6 3 2
♡ 5 4
◇ 8 2
♣ A K 5

We'll draw a veil over the bidding — suffice it to say that you are South, declarer in 6♠ and, of course, you'd like to make it. West leads the ♣Q (which, as you will learn later, you recognise as the top of a sequence).

You could have lost the ♡A on the opening lead, but you didn't, so now you have a chance to make all thirteen tricks. See if you can work it out for yourself before you look at the full deal.

Here we go, then. You win the opening lead with the ♣K in your own hand and cash the two top spades. As you can see, they

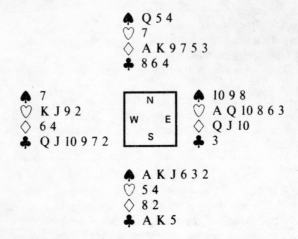

♠ Q 5 4
♡ 7
◇ A K 9 7 5 3
♣ 8 6 4

♠ 7
♡ K J 9 2
◇ 6 4
♣ Q J 10 9 7 2

♠ 10 9 8
♡ A Q 10 8 6 3
◇ Q J 10
♣ 3

♠ A K J 6 3 2
♡ 5 4
◇ 8 2
♣ A K 5

break 3-1, but most important of all, the spade queen is your only entry to dummy. So you lay off that suit and, with your fingers crossed that East has at least two diamonds, you lead a diamond. You win in dummy with the king and follow with the ace. Now you lead a third diamond and *ruff it in your own hand*. Luck has been with you, and this fells the last outstanding diamond. Now you lead a trump and win in dummy with your carefully preserved ♠Q, and you have three 'established' diamonds on which to discard your two worthless hearts and small club.

When you come to your lesson on opener's rebids you will learn that frequently he will have two suits to show and that his partner

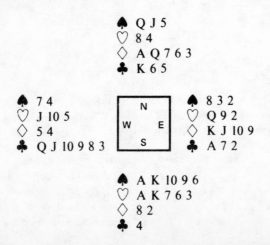

♠ Q J 5
♡ 8 4
◇ A Q 7 6 3
♣ K 6 5

♠ 7 4
♡ J 10 5
◇ 5 4
♣ Q J 10 9 8 3

♠ 8 3 2
♡ Q 9 2
◇ K J 10 9
♣ A 7 2

♠ A K 10 9 6
♡ A K 7 6 3
◇ 8 2
♣ 4

will see to it that the contract ends up in the suit which mutually fits their hands best. Here South has spades and hearts and North, who prefers spades, has seen to it that spades are trumps and the contract 4♠, against which West leads the ♣Q. Now take your time to think.

Whatever you play from dummy you're going to lose the first trick and a second club will be led on which you have to part with a trump if you want the trick — which you do. You have already seen that the best you can hope for from the spades is a 3-2 break and if you draw trumps, what are you going to do about your small hearts? You've already lost a club trick, the diamond finesse may well be wrong (which it is), and you can't afford two more losers.

You can't risk the diamond finesse at this stage as you could well get a third club led back, which would reduce your trump length still more, so you realise that your only chance is to try to set up, or 'establish' the hearts. Having ruffed the second club, then, you cash the ♡A-K and lead a third heart, *ruffing high in dummy,* just in case East has only a doubleton heart and can over-ruff the ♠5. However, Lady Luck is with you tonight, the hearts break 3-3, and you now draw the rest of the trumps ending in your own hand and play off the two good hearts. After that you can afford to take the diamond finesse in the hope of making another overtrick, but it doesn't come off and you end up making five trumps in your own hand, an extra trump in the 'short' hand, four hearts and the ♢A for an overtrick!

Now suppose the hand had been like this:

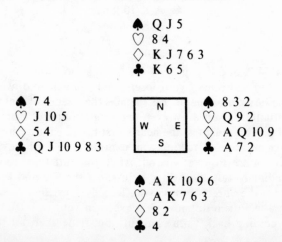

You get the same club lead against your 4♠ contract, and if you blindly draw trumps before setting up your hearts, you will go down instead of making your contract, because you can't avoid losing a club and two diamonds as well as the ♡Q.

There are a lot of lessons to be learned from this hand — please learn them all. You have ruffed a club, a suit in which you had a singleton, you have turned five trumps facing three into six tricks by thinking before you leaped into drawing trumps, you have established your hearts and, in fact, made your contract with an over-trick, whereas a lesser player could well have made only ten tricks.

May we repeat what we told you earlier in this lesson — the golden rule about drawing trumps is not golden at all. Learn to make the most of what Lady Luck has given you.

Life isn't always so rosy for you, but you can often get over the difficulties if you will only put on your thinking-cap before you rush into action. Look at this variation of the hand. Now the

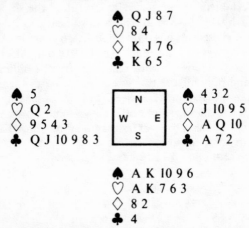

```
              ♠ Q J 8 7
              ♡ 8 4
              ◇ K J 7 6
              ♣ K 6 5

♠ 5                          ♠ 4 3 2
♡ Q 2            N           ♡ J 10 9 5
◇ 9 5 4 3     W     E        ◇ A Q 10
♣ Q J 10 9 8 3    S          ♣ A 7 2

              ♠ A K 10 9 6
              ♡ A K 7 6 3
              ◇ 8 2
              ♣ 4
```

hearts break 4-2, and if you draw the trumps too soon you will only be able to ruff one of your losers, and you will go down in what should be a certain game. Foresight is the essence of making 4♠ on this hand. If you draw even one single round of trumps, you've had it. You must test the hearts first because if they break 5-1 you have no hope of making your contract unless all the diamond honours are in West's hand. After you ruff that second club, immediately test the hearts by cashing the ace and king. When you see the queen drop on your left, all is revealed. Lead a third heart and ruff in dummy. *Don't* shorten your own trumps further by coming back via a club ruff, but remember our rule

about using a trump to get back to your own hand if this is convenient — don't shorten both hands in trumps if you can possibly
avoid it. Now back in your own hand, ruff another heart, which
establishes your last one, and you can get back to your own hand,
draw the last trump, and the thirteenth heart is good for the tenth
trick. What a simple game this is!

There is another lesson we could get from this hand which is
called *unblocking*. This simply means having the foresight to see
that you don't win a trick in the wrong hand because you haven't
got a higher one in your own hand with which you can 'overtake'.
But this has been a difficult lesson for you and we don't want to
try to stuff your heads with so much that you absorb none of it, so
we will leave this till later. Meanwhile try to make sure you really
understand this business of 'suit establishment', because you will
find time and again that it is the key to success in making your contract. Go back over the chapter and work through every hand
again, either on your own or with your tutor. Go back too over
Lesson 2, and you will see that what we were really teaching you
there was the art of 'suit establishment', though without trumps to
help you.

Compare the two types of play. With trumps you can often 'ruff
out' losers. Without trumps — playing in No Trumps — you can
only get rid of losers by allowing the opposition to win with them.
Take the first example in this lesson where you had ◇ A-K-9-7-5-3
facing ◇ 8-2. With trumps at your disposal you could play the
◇A-K, lead a third diamond and ruff it, and all the rest were
good. In No Trumps you would have had to play the ace and king
and then a small diamond which you could not win. That's why
it's so important to learn to find either a 'trump fit' or that all your
suits are guarded for play in No Trumps. We'll go on to that in
another lesson.

6 Simple Responding bids and No Trump limit-bid responses

Responding at the 1-level — responding at the 2-level — changing the suit — limit-bid responses in No Trumps — 1 NT — 2 NT — 3 NT

In Lesson 4 we told you about suit limit-bid responses which are strictly confined to hands on which your partner has opened the bidding with one of a suit *and you have four of his suit*. You will, of course, have realised that there are many, many responding hands which don't contain the requirements for a suit limit bid, but before we go on to them, just turn back to p. 26 in Lesson 4 and refresh your memories from the little box as to what these values are.

As we mentioned briefly in Lesson 4, lacking the requirements for a suit limit bid we can, if the hand is suitable, 'change the suit', that is, respond in another suit, but, as you will already have guessed, there are rules about how to do this.

You may bid any 4-card suit at the 1-level provided you have at least six points (1♡-1♠) but to 'change the suit' when you have to do so at the 2-level (1♡-2◇) promises at least eight points. It is also an absolutely golden rule that you must never bid hearts at the 2-level (1♠-2♡) without at least a 5-card heart suit. There's one other important point before we go on to look at examples, and that is that responder's change of suit is forcing — it forces partner to speak again — unless you have previously passed, and this can affect your response. For example:

♠ K Q 8 2
♡ 7 4
♢ Q 9 8 5
♣ 8 6 3

Here, as you learned in Lesson 4, if partner in first or second seat opens 1♢, your correct response is 1♠, which may help towards a No Trump contract, whilst you don't in the least mind if he repeats his diamonds. But you wouldn't have opened the bidding on this hand, so if partner, after you have passed, opens 1♢ and you bid 1♠, he could well pass and leave you to play there when the hand actually 'belongs' in diamonds. It is, therefore, wiser to make your limit bid of 2♢ in this situation rather than to change the suit to spades.

a) ♠ 9 8 4
♡ 7 6 3
♢ A J 9 7 3
♣ 6 5

b) ♠ 9 8 5
♡ 7 6 3
♢ A Q J 7 3
♣ K 7

c) ♠ 9 8 4
♡ 7 6 3
♢ A Q J 7
♣ 6 5 3

Holding hand (a), whichever suit partner opens, you haven't enough to speak. Never forget that a bid promises a minimum number of points and that opener will rely on them. Don't tell a lie. If you haven't got the points, *pass*. Here you have only 5 points. You will learn later on that opener too has his obligations. If he has better than a one-level opening he will say so, and when he doesn't and you have virtually nothing, the sooner your side steps out of the auction, the better.

With hand (b) you have 10 points. If partner opens 1♣ you can bid 1♢, but you also have enough points to bid 2♢ if he opens either 1♡ or 1♠. With hand (c) you can bid 1♢ in response to an opening bid of 1♣, but you *can't* bid 2♢ over one of either major suit. What are you to do? To pass with seven points is unthinkable but, as usual, we have a very simple solution for you, and this is to make a *limit bid* of 1 NT.

No Trump limit bids in response: The most important thing to remember about a limit bid is that it is just what it says it is, a bid which *limits* your hand. You say to partner, 'I have not less than so many points, and not more than so many, and I shan't bid again unless you make a "forcing" bid (that is, a bid which must be answered).' As usual, it is very simple to understand.

In a responding hand unsuitable for either a suit limit bid or a change-of-suit response:
With 0-5 points pass ('No Bid')
With 6-9 points bid 1 NT
With 10-12 points bid 2 NT
With 13-15 points bid 3 NT

Notice that these point counts are exactly the same as the ones given in Lesson 4, p. 26, except that the message is different. You have no particular suit you want to show, you haven't got 4-card trump support for partner's suit, and also as we told you on p. 26 we shall tell you later on something more scientific to do with a 13-15 point hand, but for now stick to the little table. We can also repeat that, once again, someone will be asking what to do with sixteen or more points. Don't worry — this will come all in good time.

There's one other little point to remember, and you shouldn't find it difficult when you're told the logic of it. If any 4-card suit is biddable, as responder you can bid one of any other suit over an opening bid of 1♣ rather than make a limit bid. For this reason we keep a response of 1 NT as a much more positive affair than it is over any other suit opening, and use it to show 8-10 points in a balanced hand. Compare these examples, and you will see that you have a perfectly sensible response on each of them.

a) ♠ K 9 3   b) ♠ K 9 8   c) ♠ K 9 3
   ♡ K 10 7 4   ♡ 10 9 7 5   ♡ K 10 7
   ◇ 10 7 5   ◇ K 9 7   ◇ J 9 7 6 2
   ♣ 10 8 2   ♣ Q 6 3   ♣ 9 3

On (a), if partner opens 1♠, you respond 1NT. Remembering that tens are a 'plus' asset, you have 6 very good points — far too good to pass in case partner has opened on a maximum hand and needs little help for game. If he opens 1♡ you raise to 2♡, as the hand falls within the range for a single raise, 6-9 points and 4-card trump support. If partner opens 1◇ you can respond 1♡, not concealing your 4-card major. If partner opens 1♣ you must on no account fall into the trap of bidding 1NT, which would show 8-10 points as before.

On hand (b) again you have a sensible response whatever partner opens. If he bids 1♣ or 1◇ bid 1♡. If he bids 1♠ bid 1NT to show your 6-9 points (*not* showing a 4-card heart suit over 1♠). If he opens 1♡ your correct response is to raise to 2♡.

On hand (c) if partner opens one of either major suit, you respond 1 NT. *Don't* be tempted to bid 2◇, as this would be promising a minimum of eight points, which you haven't got. If he opens 1◇ you have a clear-cut raise to 2 ◇ (and don't forget that, as responder with the excellent trump support, you can count one point for the doubleton club). If partner opens 1♣ you haven't got enough to bid 1 NT (8-10 points) but can bid 1◇.

2 NT response: Now let's consider responding hands on which you have a few more points. Although essentially every bid you make is exchanging information with your partner, you must remember that the opponents will be listening carefully too, so if you have a hand which you feel sure is destined to end up being played in No Trumps, it is often wiser not to help your opponents by bidding all your suits, some of which may be quite meagre, but to respond in No Trumps immediately to avoid pin-pointing the one suit of which you haven't got complete control. What we call science-fictionists, and even internationals, often make life easy for the opening leader (the player on declarer's left) to know where to strike first. One example should suffice. Using a complicated artificial system, one bidder can ask the other whether he has control of such-and-such a suit. If the answer is negative and, as the leader, you haven't got this suit, it's a matter of simple deduction that partner has it. Bridge is such a simple game!

A word of warning before we look at these stronger No Trump responding hands. For reasons which you will learn at a more advanced stage it is seldom wise to conceal a reasonable 4-card spade suit — by 'reasonable' we mean a 4-card suit headed by an honour. Someone in the class is promptly going to ask why, so as we don't believe in refusing reasons at any time, let's just say briefly that there are occasions on which not mentioning that you have four spades could mean missing a 4-4 spade fit, in which it could be safer to play than in No Trumps. We shall be going more fully into this in Lesson 8, when we discuss your choice of opening bid when you have more than one suit to show, and how you deal with this on your opener's rebid. On now, then, to stronger responding hands, again with no particular suit, other than possibly spades, which you want to show.

a) ♠ K J 8   b) ♠ A Q 10 7   c) ♠ 7 6 4 2
   ♡ K J 8 7   ♡ K 6 3   ♡ K Q 8
   ◇ K 7 4   ◇ Q 7 5 4   ◇ K J 9
   ♣ 10 9 8   ♣ 8 4   ♣ Q 8 4

On hand (a) if partner opens 1♠ you respond 2 NT. You will remember we said just now that you can never bid hearts at the 2-level without a 5-card suit, so no question of bidding 2♡ arises, and your hand falls into the 10-12 point category required for this bid. If partner opens 1♡ you have, of course, a 3♡ limit-bid response, but if he opens either 1◇ or 1♣ it is better to show your values immediately, and give away as little as possible, by bidding 2 NT. Besides getting a high bid in quickly, and possibly making life difficult for the next bidder, who may be longing to bid a suit to indicate a lead, this is a typical hand with which you would prefer the lead to come *up* to you rather than *through* you.

On hand (b) respond to 1♡, 1◇, or 1♣ with 1♠. You have the points for 2 NT, and you could also be tempted to raise 1◇ to 3◇. Neither would be wise and the best response is 1♠. It won't obstruct anything on the next round and it may be the one thing partner wants to hear.

On hand (c) if partner opens 1♠, raise to 3♠. You have the necessary 10-12 count, plus four trumps. In response to one of any other suit, bid 1♠, as you should never conceal a 4-card major which you can bid at the one-level.

3 NT response: This response we make, as has been already explained, on an evenly balanced hand of 13-15 points — just that much stronger than the 2 NT responses we have already examined. But in practice we keep this bid for hands on which no other will really do, because 13-15 points is a reasonably strong hand in itself and if it is facing a partner who has a strong opener, there may well be a slam available. An immediate jump to 3 NT may now make the subsequent bidding, if it is to go on to a slam, somewhat difficult. Remember too that if you have 13-15 points, you have an opening bid facing an opening bid, which should mean at least a certain game. It also means that you already know you and your partner have the balance of the points between you, so that there is not the same urgency to obstruct your opponents' possible bidding.

a) ♠ K J 7   b) ♠ K J 7   c) ♠ K J 7 4
   ♡ A J 6   ♡ A J 6   ♡ A J 6
   ◇ J 8 5 4   ◇ J 8 5 4   ◇ J 8 4
   ♣ J 7 2   ♣ A 7 2   ♣ A 7 2

On hand (a) you have 11 points, and would raise partner's opening of 1◇ to 3◇. This, though a non-forcing limit bid, is used to encourage opener to convert to 3 NT if he can. If the opening is 1♣, 1♡ or 1♠, bid a direct 2 NT.

Hand (b) contains 14 points and is a 'must' for a game contract facing an opening bid. It is, therefore, too good for 1◇-3◇ which could be passed and is a typical hand for an immediate response of 3 NT whatever the opening bid. Facing a 1♣ opening you might consider temporising with 1◇, but as we pointed out in earlier examples, it is a hand well fitted for No Trump play, and one where you would like the lead to come up to, rather than through your 'tenace' holdings. A 'tenace' in bridge language, by the way, is a broken honour holding such as you have in hearts and spades.

Hand (c) also contains 14 points, but if partner opens 1♣, 1◇ or 1♡, it is better to bid 1♠ than 3NT. After all, the change of suit is forcing so partner will bid again, and you can always make sure of reaching game by your later bidding. If he opens 1♠ you are too strong for a mere 3♠ (10-12 points), and until later in your studies should bid 4♠ direct.

Many students have asked why it is not permitted to respond to 1♠ with 2♡ unless you have a 5-card heart suit. The reason is that, in showing hearts, you are denying four spades and offering an alternative major as the possible trump suit. It can greatly facilitate opener's rebid if, knowing for sure that responder has five hearts, he can raise on 3-card heart support.

7 Unblocking, Ducking and Holding Up

Unblocking, what it means and why you must watch for situations where it is necessary — ducking, the difficult art of losing a trick you could win — holding up, another refusal to win, and why

---

Your tutor will, of course, have been giving you prepared hands to illustrate the lectures at each lesson, so you will already have been practising some of the things you have been taught. However, you won't want to get bogged down on bidding, so let's take another step towards learning to play the hand. In this lesson we deal with three simple techniques.

Unblocking: This may sound terrifying to beginners' ears, but it is actually as simple as pie — as simple as the game of Contract Bridge really is, and the sooner you get these procedures under your belt, the better.

The art of unblocking is nothing more nor less than making sure you can make use of all the possible goodies in your hand or dummy. Let's take a very obvious example first. Suppose you have a club suit (playing in No Trumps) divided like this:

♣ A K 9 7 6 5 2

♣ Q 8 3

You have no outside entry to dummy (North) and counting the clubs you see that there are only three against you which must fall on your own three top ones. There's really no problem about playing this suit at all, but time and again beginners make it into a problem. They play the ♣A-K and then lead a third club which *must* be won in the South hand with the ♣Q. That's South's last club, so now nothing but a helicopter will get declarer back into dummy to use the remaining four clubs for discards.

Change the scenery a little, remembering that once again, there is no other entry to dummy:

◇ A K 8 7 6 5

◇ Q 10 9 2

It would be terribly easy thoughtlessly to play the ◇A-K from the North hand and then find yourself stuck with the ◇Q-10 so that you would have, once again, no way back to dummy if you hadn't got a helicopter. As usual, there's an easy way of dealing with the situation as long as you *think* before you play a card.

To 'unblock', that is, to provide yourself with a helicopter, play the high card or cards from the 'short' hand first.

The 'short' hand is nothing more nor less than the hand with the shorter holding, in both these examples South. So on the first example you are careful to play the ♣Q from your own hand first, so that you have two small ones left and, after cashing the ♣A-K, you will be in dummy to run the rest of the clubs without obstruction.

In the second example it's not enough to be careful to play the ◇Q first because if you next play your ◇2 to dummy, the ◇2 and ◇9 will fall on the ◇A-K, but you will be stuck with the ◇10 which can't help winning the fourth diamond trick. You have to remember our golden rule, to play the high cards from the short hand first. Try to work it out — got it? Yes, you play first the ◇Q on which you put dummy's ◇5. Next you play the ◇10 and overtake it with the ◇K. The vital move comes next — you must play

your ◇9 on dummy's ◇A, leaving yourself with the ◇2 which
won't snatch the trick away from the run of established diamonds.

♡ A Q J 7 4
◇ A Q J

♡ K 3
◇ 7 2
♣ A 7 4 2

There's no reason why you shouldn't learn to use your cards to
full advantage, so let's take things one step further. Here's part of
the dummy and your own hand. Without the diamonds you
would be very careful to play the ♡K from the short hand —
South — first, so that you would have the ♡3 left to lead to
dummy and, if the suit breaks no worse than 4-2, you would take
five heart tricks. Now you have the diamond finesse to consider.
(Turn back to Lesson 2 if you want to revise what a finesse is all
about.) Remember that if you play off the ◇A you are just asking
for the enemy to make a diamond trick, whoever has the ◇K. So
you want to lead *from* your nothing, the ◇7-2, *towards* your
something, the ◇A-Q-J. Lead a low diamond and finesse the ◇J
on the half-and-half chance that West holds the king. If this finesse holds, return to your own hand by playing a low heart to your
♡K. This has the double effect of getting rid of the high card from
the 'short' hand, and giving you an entry to your own hand to
repeat the diamond finesse. Once with three diamond tricks safely
under your belt you can now run off the rest of the hearts without
any danger of 'blocking' them, and discarding three losing clubs
as you do so.

Ducking: This time we're back to that most difficult thing for
learners to do, and that is deliberately to lose a trick when you
needn't, but this will be because you have developed an eye to the
future.

These situations generally crop up when you are short of entries
to one hand or the other. Imagine you are playing the hand in No

◇ A K 8 6 2

◇ 7 5 4

Trumps and this diamond suit is dummy's only asset. There are five diamonds missing, so it is inconceivable that you could get away with less than one loser in the suit. If you had an outside entry to dummy you could play off the ◇A-K and then a third diamond, bravely letting the opponents win, and then use the outside entry to get back to your established ◇6-2. Without that entry, this plan would only work if you'd got your helicopter with you so what you have to do is create one of your own. Play a small diamond from your own hand and *duck* it, that is, play a small diamond from dummy too. Mad? *No!* Because now if the outstanding diamonds break 3-2, you will lose the first diamond trick, but the remaining cards in the suit will fall when you next get in and lead one of your remaining diamonds to dummy, cash the ◇A-K, and play off the other two.

♠ A K Q 7 3

♠ 6 5 4

With a holding such as this *plus* a certain entry to dummy, you can afford to play off the ♠A-K-Q and to hope that the opponents' five break 3-2. If they don't you will only make four tricks in the suit, but the entry will allow you to get at the last one. *Without* a sure entry you will have to employ your ducking technique again unless it is so vital for you to win all five tricks that you've got to take the risk of playing off the three tops first. If you can make your contract with only four spade tricks, then safeguard the situation, at the same time manufacturing that helicopter, by playing a small spade and *ducking* it. Now you will be able to get back to the North hand to play the fourth spade even if someone started with ♠J-x-x-x.

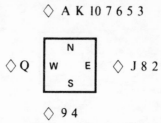

$\diamondsuit$ A K 10 7 6 5 3

$\diamondsuit$ Q $\diamondsuit$ J 8 2

$\diamondsuit$ 9 4

We'll look at just one more example of how vital this technique can be. Here is the whole of the diamond suit from a hand which South is playing in 6♠. The rest of the cards don't matter. Suffice it to say that South can win West's opening lead and draw trumps, but he can only afford to lose one trick. This in turn means that he must win at least six diamond tricks. He has no entry to dummy other than his two diamonds, but do you see what will happen if he leads one from his own hand and thoughtlessly plays the $\diamondsuit$ K when West produces the $\diamondsuit$ Q? The $\diamondsuit$ A-K will win, but East's $\diamondsuit$ J will be the best diamond for the third diamond trick and South, without a helicopter, will be left staring dismally at four good diamonds in dummy.

It's true that *if* the outstanding diamonds broke 2-2, South could safely play his two on the $\diamondsuit$ A-K and not lose a single trick in the suit. But this is against the mathematical odds, and it is more likely that one opponent will have one diamond and the other three. Don't ask what happens if they break 4-0 because the sad answer is that you'll go down in your contract.

Holding Up: This is not to be confused with ducking though in a way the techniques are rather similar. Holding up means refusing to win an opposition's trick when you could do so because, once again, you have an eye to the future. We are only going to touch the fringes of the subject here, but it is very important and, strange as it may seem, it is a technique which crops up, especially in declarer play of a No Trump contract, more often than any other.

Here is a part of your hand. You are playing in No Trumps and West has led a heart. You will learn all in good time that West will have attacked in his longest and strongest suit. Right at the beginning of Lesson 2 we told you about keeping your guards in the opponents' suit — this time you've got to do it for a different reason.

West attacks by leading a heart which we will take it is from a 5-card suit, which will mean that East has three hearts. But let's sup-

♡ 7 5
◇ A Q J 9 2

♡ A K 4
◇ 8 7 3

pose that you are missing one of the black aces — which is held by East — and that he also has the ◇K. You'll have to finesse the diamonds — in hope, which doesn't come off — and you'll have to tackle that black suit. Each time he gets in, East will return his partner's lead, a heart, and if you have played the ♡K at trick 1 and your second high heart next time East leads the suit, you will have nothing but a small one left, and nothing you can do will prevent East from leading his third heart, which will mean three heart tricks for West. It's a very different matter if you *hold up* your ♡A-K at trick 1. East will probably win and lead a second heart. This time you will win and get going with your diamonds, but you still have a heart guard which you can use on the third round and East, devoid of hearts after that, will be unable to put his partner in to make his established hearts.

It is just as important, if not more so, to hold up if you reduce your heart guards to ♡A-x-x only. Hold up once, and then twice, and now East will be unable to return a heart any time later, as his three will have been exhausted. If you've used up your ♡A on either the first or second round of the suit, East will come in and unstitch you in no uncertain manner.

Rule of Seven: There's a little gimmick to help you when you have only one stop in the suit in which you are attacked as, for example, ♡A-x-x facing ♡x-x. Add together the number of cards in your hand and dummy (A-x-x + x-x = 5) and deduct from 7, = 2, so hold up twice. With A-x-x facing x-x-x you have 6. 7 − 6 = 1, so hold up once.

8 Opener's choice of bid

Two-suited hands, basic rules for opening — 4-4-4-1 hands — 4-4-3-2 hands

You have no problem to solve when, as opener *or* responder, you have just one suit to show, but life gets more difficult when you find you have two, or perhaps even three suits, which is the case if your distribution is 4-4-4-1. Let's start first with opener's bid. He hasn't got a No Trump type of hand, he hasn't got only one suit, so he has to choose between, we'll say, two suits. There are rules to guide you, but these are very flexible and must give way to common sense.

Two-Suited Hands — Opening:
  1) Bid the longer suit before the shorter.
  2) With two equal-length suits bid the higher-ranking before the lower-ranking if the suits are touching, except if they are spades and clubs, when bid clubs first.
  3) Bid the stronger suit before the weaker except if the suits are adjacent or both black.

We have deliberately not included non-touching suits in the above table (clubs and spades count as running in a circle and are, therefore, touching) because your choice here will depend on the strength of your hand.

There are two things to remember, firstly that the object of the auction is to discover which suit, if any, provides the best fit with your partner, and secondly that it is an unfortunate fact of life that partner frequently responds in the suit you like least. If he has some points but not a fit for your suit — no limit-bid raise, in fact, as he had in Lesson 4 — then he will want to show you his own suit, in the hope that you will have a fit for him, or that it will enable you to go into No Trumps. This is where judging which of two suits to bid first becomes so important, and here a third and all-important rule comes into it — a new suit bid at the three-level is *forcing,* which means that your partner *must* reply, so you must never force him into the position of bidding again if your own hand isn't strong enough to stand it. This problem doesn't arise if your two suits are adjacent, but it can very well arise if your suits are not touching ones, as we shall see from some examples. Before we get to these, remember that a 4-card suit is always biddable, but is not *rebiddable,* which means that you can't wriggle out of any awkward situations by repeating a 4-card suit. The mere fact that you bid a suit twice guarantees that it is of at least 5-card length.

a) ♠ A Q 10 9 7
   ♡ A K 10 8 4
   ◇ 7 5
   ♣ 8

b) ♠ A Q 10 9 7
   ♡ 7 5
   ◇ 8
   ♣ A K 10 8 4

c) ♠ A Q 10 9 7
   ♡ 7 5
   ◇ A K 10 8 4
   ♣ 8

Hand (a) is easy. Bid 1♠ , the higher-ranking of equal and adjacent suits, and if partner responds with two of either minor, offer your hearts as an alternative. Hand (b) is equally easy. Note that the cards are the same except in different suits. Open 1♣ because if partner responds with one of a red suit you can offer your alternative of spades at the one-level. Hand (c) is the one on which you must think. The suits are divided. If you open 1◇ and partner responds 1♡, all is well, as you can bid 1♠, but if you open 1◇ and he responds 2♣ you would have to bid 2♠ to show the suit. This is known as a 'reverse' and is reserved for a much stronger hand than you have here, about which you will learn later. So what are you to do on hand (c)? In practice a major suit is more valuable than a minor, so your wisest course would be to open 1♠. If partner responds 2♣ all is well, as you can bid 2◇, but if he responds 2♡ you are not strong enough to bid a *forcing* 3◇, so have to compromise by rebidding 2♠, which at least confirms that you have a 5-card suit.

♠ 10 8 7 5 4
♡ A K Q J 10
♢ A 6
♣ 8

What would you bid on this hand? Perhaps now you can stand the shock of being told that the correct bid is 1♠, not 1♡ because of all the pretty pictures! We've already said that the object of the auction is to discover the best fit with partner's hand and if he had, for instance, three spades and even three hearts, the heart honours are always going to be useful, and the eight spades between the two hands are going to provide a fit with — probably — the enemy honours falling together when you set out to draw trumps. Open 1♠ and rebid 2♡ if partner responds 2♢ or 2♣.

If we consider 4-4-4-1 hands next, three suits, it will help to solve many of your problems on hands where you have only two 4-card suits, so let's take the 4-4-4-1 hands. The rules are very simple:

With a 4-4-4-1 hand and all three suits 'biddable':
Bid one of the suit below the singleton unless the singleton is clubs, when bid 1♡ .
If one of the three suits is so weak that it is of value only in support if partner bids it, treat the hand as a two-suiter, to which we shall be coming in a moment.

---

a) ♠ A Q 8 7   b) ♠ A Q 8 7   c) ♠ 9 7 6 2
   ♡ A K 7 4   ♡ A K 7 4   ♡ A K J 9
   ♢ 6   ♢ K J 10 8   ♢ 6
   ♣ K J 10 8   ♣ 6   ♣ A K J 9

Before we look at the bidding of these three hands, make sure you know that with only 4-card suits, you must be fully up to strength in honour points, because you have no ruffing values until you have established a suit fit with your partner. But now to the hands themselves. With (a) you bid a simple 1♣, the suit below the singleton. If partner responds 1♢ you can bid 1♡. As no really sound bidder ever conceals a biddable spade suit, you won't be missing a spade fit. On hand (b) your singleton is in clubs, so you apply the rule which says that in this case you should open 1♡. Why? Because of what we said only a moment ago — no sound bidder ever conceals a biddable spade suit, so if partner has spades you won't miss a spade fit. However, you also learned in Lesson 6 that you must not respond at the 2-level in hearts without a 5-card suit, so if you chose to open 1♠ and partner had four hearts, he couldn't mention them and a perfect heart fit might be lost for ever. Hand (c) is an example of one where the spades are of value only if you are able to support a spade bid from partner, so treat the hand as a two-suiter in hearts and clubs.

This brings us quite simply to the hands where you have a 4-4-3-2 distribution and, therefore, only two suits to show. If the two suits are adjacent the same old rule applies, bid the higher-ranking first so that you can rebid in the lower-ranking, asking partner for 'preference'. You will learn all about this when you come to the lesson on responder's rebids so don't worry about it now.

Let's face it, unless the two suits are adjacent you can have problems, but the best and simplest rule for solving them is mentally to *demote* your doubleton and consider it as a singleton, after which apply the rules for bidding 4-4-4-1 hands. We'll have the usual little crop of examples but you'll never really know what would have been best until you see your partner's hand.

a)	♠ K Q 9 4	b)	♠ K Q 9 4	c)	♠ K Q 9 4
	♡ A K 9 2		♡ 7 5		♡ Q 8 2
	◇ Q 8 3		◇ A K 9 2		◇ 7 5
	♣ 7 5		♣ K 8 3		♣ A K 9 2

With (a) you have no problem as your two suits are adjacent. Bid 1 ♠ in the knowledge that you can rebid in hearts if partner responds in a minor. On (b) you mentally demote your doubleton heart and think of it as a singleton. Now the suit below the singleton is the diamond one, so you open 1◇. If partner bids 1♠ you've found the fit. If he bids 1♡ you can bid 1♠, and if he bids 2♣ you can do no better than raise to 3♣. With (c) you are back to the rule for bidding two black suits of equal length. Open 1♣ and bid 1♠ if partner responds in a red suit.

To end this chapter here, very briefly, are the tabulated hints on which suit to choose:

Length of suits	Bid
6-6 or 5-5	Higher-ranking of adjacent suits unless both black when open 1♣.
5-4	Try to bid the 5-card suit first. If the 4-card suit is weak, ignore it unless you can use it in support of partner.
6-5, 7-6 or 7-5	Bid longer suit first unless the suits are adjacent in a weak hand. Rebid in shorter suit, showing that it is rebiddable — i.e., at least a 5-card suit, so first bid suit must be the longer.
6-4	Bid and *rebid* 6-card suit unless the 4-card suit is a major which can be bid at the one-level, e.g., with six clubs and four hearts open 1♣ and rebid 2♣ over 1♠, but if response is 1♢, show 4-card heart suit (1♣ -1♢ -1♡).
4-4-4-1	Open one of the suit below the singleton unless the singleton is clubs, when open 1♡. If one suit is too weak to be 'biddable', ignore it and treat the hand as a two-suiter unless the weak 4-card suit can be used to support partner.
4-4-3-2	With adjacent suits bid higher-ranking first unless the suits are clubs and spades, when bid clubs first. If the suits are divided, mentally demote the doubleton to a singleton and treat as for 4-4-4-1 hands.

9   Opening Leads

Leading against suit contracts
— leading partner's bid suit
— some 'don'ts' — leading
against No Trump contracts —
the Rule of Eleven, how it works and why

You will probably have been asking for some time what you should lead on any particular hand, and doubtless your tutor has said, 'Just take it from me.' The reason for this, of course, is that you can't learn everything at once, but we think now you've got to the point where you need specific guidance, so let's get on with what is likely to be a somewhat long and difficult lesson.

The rules for leading against a suit contract or a No Trump contract are completely different. We have written a whole separate book on the subject of leading, so we can only take it briefly here, but we'll start with what is actually your first lesson on defence.

Leading Against a Suit Contract: In this case the declarer has got the power of a trump suit — the teeth which, if you aren't careful, will bite off the heads of your lovely aces and kings, all potential winners if you 'cash' them in time. Leading when partner has bid during the auction is quite different from leading 'blind', and we'll take 'blind' leads first.

If you have a sequence of two or more high honours at the head of a side-suit (not declarer's trump suit) lead the top of it. Here are some examples, with the card to lead in italics:

A-K-x-x: A-K-Q-x-x: A-K with no small cards: K-Q-J alone or with small cards: Q-J-10-x and so on.

The top of a sequence will never give away a trick, and it is also used as a signal to partner that you have at least the one below it. If, therefore, you look with suspicion at the third example, note the particular statement that your holding is A-K *bare*. Here your signal, or message, is different. When you lead the king, which holds the trick, and *follow* it with the ace, it is a signal to partner — your first lesson on partnership language — that you have no more and can ruff the third round if partner gets in in time to lead a third.

Never lead the king when you ought to lead the ace, or the queen when you ought to lead the king, as you will be giving wrong information to your partner. If you lead the king of a suit, he will *expect* you to have the queen but not the ace, and if he can see the queen either in his own hand or in dummy, he won't know what the heck you've led from!

You can see how important it is to lead top cards if possible against a suit contract, can't you? If you have a suit headed by the A-K or perhaps even A-K-Q, you have every hope of winning with them if you do so before the rats get at them.

If you haven't got a helpful-looking suit to lead, you can try to search for something in partner's hand, judging this against the bidding. You can lead 'top of nothing', that is, the 8 from a combination such as 8-7-3, but be careful to play the 7 on the second round of the suit, in the hope that partner will notice that the 3 is missing and that you, therefore, started with three and can't ruff the third round. You may lead the top of a doubleton — two cards, such as the 7 from 7-2, and if partner gets in in time he may be able to give you a third-round ruff. You can lead a singleton, as long as it's not a king or queen which might be finessed into your hand and thereby become a winner, but there's a helpful little gimmick for you here:

> The better your hand, the worse a singleton lead is.
> The worse your hand, the better a singleton lead is.

The reason is that the sole purpose of leading a singleton is to get in a ruff. If you have a good defensive hand, you are unlikely to find partner able to win a trick to give you your ruff. If you have peanuts, then partner may well be able to get in before your trumps are exhausted.

Leading Partner's Bid Suit: Learn the rules by heart — they are too important to allow yourself to make a mistake, which can not only mislead partner, but can turn out very much to declarer's advantage.

From any holding headed by partner's ace, lead the ace (*A*-x-x)
From any sequence of two or more honours, lead the top (*Q*-J-x)
From any four cards other than if you have partner's ace, lead the bottom card (*A*-8-5-3 but Q-8-5-*3* or 8-6-5-*3*)
From any three cards headed by an honour other than the ace, lead the *bottom* card (K-8-*3*, Q-7-*4*, or even J-6-*5*)
From any doubleton lead the top card (*K*-6, *Q*-4, or *J*-5)

It's a pity we haven't space to go into this interesting subject more fully, but perhaps we can spare a moment to try to dispel once and for all the myth about 'lead the highest of partner's bid suit'. You lead the ace, if you have it, to try to make sure of winning a trick with it — nothing can be more infuriating than to lead low and find declarer with the king bare or perhaps the K-x-x and a singleton in dummy so that he can win the first round and ruff the second and third. With one of the other honours at the head of a 3- or 4-card holding you lead *low*. Let's look at just a couple of examples:

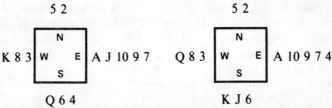

In the first example, if you lead the king, nothing can prevent South's queen from becoming the master on the third round. If you lead the 3, however, East will win with the ace and lead the knave back through declarer's remaining Q-6, allowing him no trick in the suit. The second example is even worse from a defensive point of view. If you lead the queen nothing can prevent declarer from coming to two tricks in the suit. If you lead the 3, East will go up with the ace and lead the 10 back through declarer's remaining K-J, and though he will get one winner, he won't get two.

We have been told that it is always possible to dream up examples to prove a case. Well, so we could, but there is no need to do so. The honest-to-goodness fact is that though you will meet distributions where the low lead won't help you, you will never be able to find one where, used intelligently, and with a partner likely to be able to interpret your holding. it will cost you anything.

Some Important 'Don'ts': Having given you quite a bit of help towards what you should lead, let's turn to some of the important things *not* to lead. You're back now to a 'blind' lead against a trump suit contract, and the two most important 'don'ts' are not to lead away from a tenace or an unsupported honour. We'll explain both.

A 'tenace' is a broken honour holding such as A-Q-x, K-J-x, and so on. The reason why any card, high or low, from such a holding is bad is that it can be leading right into the free gifts department for declarer. Declarer is the one with the announced balance of the values, so if you hold an A-Q combination, it is very probable that declarer has the missing king. If you touch the suit, his king will make a trick, whereas if you wait until it is led from dummy or by your partner towards your hand, your ace will be fulfilling its destiny of killing declarer's king and you may well find your queen making a trick too. In the case of leading from a K-J-x the same applies — declarer is very likely to hold the A-Q, and by leading up to, or into, his hand, you will have done all the work for him. He will no longer need to take a finesse in the hope of catching the high cards which he will be hoping are held by your partner. Similarly, you could get one of many possible combinations such as this:

A x x

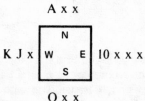

$$K J x \quad \boxed{\begin{array}{c} N \\ W \quad E \\ S \end{array}} \quad 10 \text{ x x x}$$

Q x x

If you lead low away from your K-J, South will play low from dummy and be delighted when his queen wins the trick. Later on his ace will win so the best you will get is one trick whereas, if you had held on and waited for declarer or your partner to lead the suit, your side would have won two tricks and declarer only one.

Much the same sort of positions arise if you lead *away* from unsupported honours. An unsupported honour is just one honour card at the head of a suit, such as K-x-x-x, Q-x-x-x, J-x-x-x or, worst of all, A-x-x-x. It needn't be a 4-card suit, as just the same applies to a 3- or 5-card suit. In the case of leading 'a little x' from a suit headed by the ace, not only do you risk never making your ace, but you probably cut short its destiny of killing the king. Leading away from any other unsupported honour is likely to have just the same effects as leading away from a tenace.

One of the difficulties of making learners understand the truth of this is that so often their crimes don't find them out. It is possible for example, to lead the 4 from Q-8-6-4. If declarer has the A-K-J or a combination of these in his own hand and dummy, the student will see what he has done, but if partner has even one of the touching honours, no damage will have been done, because partner's honour will protect the unsupported one in the leader's hand.

You will notice that we specifically mentioned leading from 3-, 4-, or 5-card suits. The reason for this is that, on one horrible occasion, we had used K-J-x-x to demonstrate why *not* to lead this suit. Later, when the set boards were being played, one of us saw declarer making an overtrick, which we knew to be impossible. On enquiring how on earth this had been done, we found the opening leader had led low from K-J-x-x-x. 'But you've just been told *never* to lead away from a suit headed by K-J — there it is still on the blackboard!' 'Well,' came the answer, 'you said not to lead from *four* to the K-J, and I've got five.' Remember that at no time can you afford to go into the free gifts department and hand away a trick declarer couldn't make for himself.

Leading Against No Trump Contracts: If leading against a No Trump contract when partner has bid a suit, the rules are exactly the same as for leading against a suit contract, with one exception — now you have no teeth in the form of a trump suit to fear, so can lead low from A-x-x rather than lead the ace itself. This is a very rough guideline and, as your experience grows, you will learn to modify your lead, judging it against the bidding. Far more often, however, you will be making one of those 'blind' leads we've talked about before, and here it is almost always best to attack in your longest and strongest suit. Unless you have three honours in the suit (when you should pick the one indicated in the table of standard leads on p. 196) it is customary to lead the fourth best — fourth from the top, not fourth up from the bottom. So if you decide to attack in hearts from a suit such as ♡K-J-8-6-5, you would lead the ♡6.

You may notice that this conflicts entirely with the rule on p. 56 of this lesson, where we told you not to lead away from a suit headed by a tenace, but there's all the difference in the world. This time you have no declarer 'teeth' to fear and are, in fact, hoping to set up, or establish, your own small cards so that you may drive out declarer's guards in the suit and later make winners out of your own small cards. If you are lucky enough to find partner with the ♡ A, or even the ♡ Q, half the battle is won, but at least he will know the suit in which you *hope* to set up winners and, if he gets in during the play, he will know which suit to lead back to you.

The fourth best of your longest and strongest suit — why the fourth best? This brings us to the vitally important . . .

Rule of Eleven: Admittedly declarer can make use of this rule but, on balance, it is better to put partner in the picture as quickly as possible. When you lead a fourth best, partner deducts the pip number of the card led, in our example of ♡ 6, from eleven, and the answer, here 11 - 6 = 5, gives him the number of cards *higher* than the card led which are divided between dummy, his own hand, and declarer's.

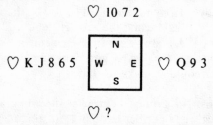

♡ 10 7 2

♡ K J 8 6 5   N W E S   ♡ Q 9 3

♡ ?

Lead, ♡ 6. There are two higher in dummy, the ♡ 10-7 and East has the ♡ Q-9 so that four of the missing five are visible. Declarer, therefore, has only one heart higher than the ♡ 6, and when East has seen it, he has seen it once and for all. On many occasions this can be exceptionally helpful to the defence.

We have found that many students, particularly those with inquiring mathematical minds, want to know *why* this rule always works and are not content to leave it to trust. Here, then, briefly, is the 'why'.

A normal suit runs A 2 3 4 5 6 7 8 9 10 J Q K, but we are playing bridge, where the ace counts as the highest card. So we remove it from its lowly place and reconstitute the suit as 2 3 4 5 6 7 8 9 10 J Q K A. Now give those pretty pictures at the top of the suit numbers instead of names, and we get:

2 3 4 5 6 7 8 9 10 11 12 13 14)
J Q K A)

The player who led his fourth best of a suit is known to hold three higher cards than the one he led, so mentally knock off the 12th, 13th, and 14th, and that leaves you with the mystical number, *eleven.*

If it gives you nightmares at first, don't worry — accept the Rule of Eleven as fact. But take it to bed with you and think about it, and light will surely dawn. If you still can't understand *why,* then just use the rule and all you can get from it.

Remember to lead the top of a sequence, that is, the top of a run of three touching cards, if you have it, not the fourth best. Suppose you held Q-J-10-8-6 of the suit in which you propose to attack. Lead the queen, not the fourth best which would be the 8. The top of a sequence won't give away a trick, whereas if you lead the 8, and declarer happens to hold A-K-9 you have rushed straight into the free gifts department and given him a trick with his 9 which he could never have got for himself. It's true partner won't be able to do sums about the situation of missing cards, but he will recognise the top of a sequence for what it is, and will get just as much information from it.

Finally, if you go out from your class into the big wide world, don't allow yourself to be bamboozled out of the correct facts you have learned. The two you will find most often hurled at your head are that from A-K-Q combinations you should lead the king, not the ace, and that you should always lead the highest of partner's bid suit. These two ideas went out with the ark, so stick to your guns in the knowledge that you have been taught modern methods which have extremely good reasons behind them, and that if you are playing in company which hasn't caught up with them yet, you can judge the standard of your opposition.

10 The Stayman Convention

*A convention — the Stayman 2 ♣ Convention —
how it got its name — when to use it — opener's 2♢
response — the next step by responder — and by
opener*

This is the first time we have mentioned the word 'convention' to
you. Don't be frightened because it's very simple. A convention is,
quite simply, a bid which doesn't mean what it sounds as though it
means. In Contract Bridge we use many of these, but as far as you
are concerned you'll work up to the rather more complicated ones
gradually. The simple ones, which are all that you will need to con-
cern yourselves about, were developed because people saw the
need to find bids to show specific values or ask specific questions
during the auction. As you aren't allowed to ask your partner
whether he has so and so, or tell him directly that you have so and
so, you have to do it by way of a conventional bid, and for the
most part bids which have very little use in their natural sense
have been extracted and turned into conventional ones.

If you will turn back to Lesson 3 and refresh your memories
about the weak take-out responses to a No Trump opening bid,
you will see that we said that you could make a weak take-out, if
you considered your hand unsuitable for play in the No Trumps
your partner had suggested, by simply bidding 2♢, 2♡, or 2♠,
and at this point we said categorically that you could not make a
weak take-out into 2♣ as this had a special meaning. Now we're
really coming to it — a 2♣ response to 1 NT is conventional, that
is, it doesn't mean what it sounds as though it means. It is the 'Stayman Convention', which we use to find out whether opener has a 4-
card major suit. We shall make it very simple for you — bridge is a

simple game. But first a word about how it got its name.

How the Stayman Convention Got Its Name: Everyone knows the American genius for advertising, though nowadays we're not lagging far behind. Anyway, the use of a bid of 2♣ in response to an opening 1 NT as a suit fit-finding bid was invented by the immortal British International Ewart Kempson and refined by him and another British International, Jack Marx. Sam Stayman came over here, met the convention and saw it in action. He took it back to America because he was so impressed with it, wrote a book about it, added a lot of frilly bits, and called it 'the Stayman 2♣'. We're not going to bother about the frilly bits, only the main convention and when and how to use it.

The Stayman 2♣ Convention: This is a bid of 2♣ facing a 1 NT opening bid. It doesn't mean you want to make a weak take-out into clubs but *does* mean that you would like to know whether your partner has a 4-card major suit because, knowing the magic of a 4-4 trump suit fit (remember that 8 cards between two hands should give you control of the suit?) and because of the make-up of your own hand, you feel life would be safer if the hand were played in spades or hearts rather than No Trumps. In such circumstances you *ask* opener about the make-up of *his* hand by bidding 2♣ rather than making a take-out or a direct raise immediately.

There is one vital rule to learn at this point, and once you've got that firmly fixed in your minds you'll find the rest simple:

Never bid a Stayman 2♣ unless you have worked out that you have a sensible course of action you can take on the next round, whatever opener's reply.

There are also a few simple but equally vital rules for opener, who has to answer his partner's 2♣ question:

1) With no 4-card major suit, bid 2◇ irrespective of the actual point count of your hand or your diamond holding.
2) Holding one 4-card major, bid it at the 2-level (1 NT - 2♣ - 2♡) and leave the next step to partner.
3) Holding two 4-card majors, show the hearts first. (This is a matter of partnership agreement and some top-class partnerships prefer to show the spades first.)

Responder, when he has heard the reply to his question, can take various courses of action:

1) If opener's answer suits his hand, he can pass or raise, according to his strength.

2) If the rebid does *not* suit his hand he can now make a weak take-out, that is, bid a suit at the two-level, which he could have done in the first place if he hadn't taken the trouble to inquire about the possibility of a fit in either major, or make a jump bid in his own suit (1 NT – 2♣ – 2♦ – 3♠) showing an interest in a game contract in spite of the unsatisfactory answer to his question, or take back into 2 NT or 3 NT, according to strength.

By now someone is going to be asking what happens if you really want to make a weak take-out into clubs. As usual the answer is simple. Respond 2♣ to the opening 1 NT. Opener will reply on the assumption that you are making a conventional Stayman inquiry, and you now bid 3♣ to show you didn't really mean it at all! Some people will ask you why you couldn't just bid 3♣ in the first place, but again the answer is simple — a jump bid in a suit facing an opening No Trump is forcing to game, so you must have a means of distinguishing for your partner whether you have a game-going hand based on clubs or one on which you would like to make a weak take-out. Be rather wary of using this weak club sequence, remembering that it is going to commit you to playing at the 3-level, so you would never use it on less than a 6-card suit.

Before we go into examples, there is another important point to remember, and that is that it doesn't matter what strength of No Trump you are using as long as you and your partner (not to mention the opposition) know what it is. Currently we are working on a 12-14-point No Trump, but if you are playing 'strong' (which we shall teach you later) you simply gear your bids to the knowledge of the greater number of points your partner is promising.

As usual, example hands will help to clear the fog completely but keep referring back to the rules and to Lesson 3 to make sure you know what we are talking about.

	a)	b)	c)
♠	10 9 6 4	K 10 8 7 6 2	J 8
♡	J 8 5 3	9 5 4	J 10 7 6
♦	A 8 6	8 6	A 9 8 7 4 2
♣	5 4	5 4	5

These first three hands are definitely 'don't' for the use of Stayman. Just because you've learned a new gadget, don't use it on every hand! On hand (a), apply the test of asking yourself what you can do if you bid 2♣ in an attempt to find a 4-card heart or spade fit, and partner responds 2◇. Nothing you can do but shoot yourself before partner does it, is there? You can't make a weak take-out into no better than a 4-card suit at *any* time and you can't rebid 2 NT if you get that unsatisfactory 2◇ rebid because (Lesson 3) you haven't enough points to raise 1 NT to 2 NT in the first place, and that is what you would mean you had if you bid 2 NT now — in other words, 1 NT – 2♣ – 2 ◇ – 2 NT is *out*. There's no question of using Stayman on hand (b). You don't want to *ask* partner anything, but to tell him by bidding 2♠, a weak take-out, that you are not interested in anything but a low level contract in spades. Hand (c) is rather a special case, but definitely not suitable for a 2♣ question because you can't find an answer when you ask yourself what you would do on the next round *whatever* opener rebids. If he responds 2◇ (no 4-card major) you could pass, knowing that his opening bid must contain at least two diamonds and that you will be giving him six. If he responds 2♡ you are happy because you've found a 4-4 heart fit, and on this meagre point count you would pass. But you completely failed to find an answer when you asked yourself what you would do if he replied to 2♣ with 2♠. You must, therefore, satisfy yourself with an immediate weak take-out into 2◇, which you know partner will pass.

One other 'don't' is don't use Stayman when you have an evenly balanced hand perfectly suitable for play in No Trumps such as this. There is unlikely to be any advantage from playing in a 4-4

♠ Q 10 8
♡ K J 9 4
◇ Q 9 7
♣ Q J 6

heart fit, you have 'something in everything' and the count to raise 1 NT invitationally to 2 NT. Add, say, the ♡Q in place of the ♡4, and you would raise to 3 NT direct.

Now let's turn to some hands which *are* suitable for a Stayman 2♣ bid.

a) ♠ J 8 7 4   b) ♠ K Q 8 7   c) ♠ K J 9
   ♡ Q J 9 6 5   ♡ 9 2   ♡ Q 9 8 2
   ◇ 8 6 5   ◇ Q J 10 8   ◇ K 8 6 4
   ♣ 6   ♣ K Q 7   ♣ Q 8

On hand (a), really weak, you can see little future for poor partner left to struggle in No Trumps, and would far prefer to play in spades or hearts if partner has a 4-card fit for either. Bid 2♣ facing partner's opening 1 NT, and if he responds 2♠ or 2♡, pass happily. If he responds 2◇, denying a 4-card major, rebid 2♡, which is just as much the weak take-out it would have been if you'd bid it in the first place, except that you grabbed your opportunity to ask if he had four spades *or* four hearts. On hand (b) you have ample to raise 1 NT to 3 NT, but are just a trifle worried about those weak hearts. Bid 2♣ and if partner rebids 2♠, raise him to 4♠. If he rebids 2♡, you know he has four of them, so can rebid 3 NT without fear. If he rebids 2◇, denying a 4-card major, you will have to take your life in your hands, because you know he can't have more than three spades or hearts, but equally you know that you have enough points to be in a game contract, so you must risk the hearts. With hand (c) you have enough to raise 1 NT to an invitational 2 NT, but if partner should have a 4-card heart fit for you, you feel this might well be safer than No Trumps. Bid 2♣ and if partner rebids 2♠ you will know that he hasn't got four hearts, so will simply bid 2 NT, announcing your point count, which you could have done without going through the motions of 'Stayman', except that you took your chance to find out about a possible heart fit. If he responds 2◇, denying four cards in either major, rebid 2 NT, again announcing your point count and making an invitational bid which partner could pass or raise according to his own strength, which can't be less than 12 points or more than 14. If he responds 2♡, now you have found your 4-4 fit. Raise his 2♡ to 3♡, invitationally, telling him that you need him to have a good to maximum No Trump opening before he decides to go on to 4♡.

For experienced players there are many more extensions to the 2♣ fit-finding convention but you need not worry about them until you have been playing for very much longer. In the meantime if you decide, as you certainly should do, to play this convention, make sure your partner knows it too. Never forget to ask yourself that vital question whether you have a sensible course of action to take whatever reply you get to your 2♣ bid, and never tell a lie about your values after you've heard the reply to your 2 ♣ bid. In other words, if you're not too keen on the rebid and decide to go back into No Trumps, don't bid 2 NT if your hand is worth 3 NT, or you may well miss a game. Conversely, if your hand is only worth a 2 NT rebid, don't rebid 3 NT. In the same way, if opener's rebid hits the jackpot of the suit you would like to play in, pass if your combined values don't reach game, give an invitational raise from the 2-level to the 3-level if you are hopeful but slightly doubtful about game unless partner is maximum, but never leave him on the hook of guessing if you *know* you ought to be in game — bid it yourself.

Many's the first-class contract you will reach by way of the Stayman Convention which you couldn't have bid without it.

Jump Take-Out in a Minor: There's one other thing you should learn on the subject of responding to 1 NT. On p. 21 we explained the jump take-out in the majors (♡ and ♠), but there is a difference if your suit is a minor (◇ or ♣). 1 NT – 3♡/♠ is unconditionally forcing to game, but 1 NT – 3◇/♣ is also unconditionally forcing, but also invitational to a slam.

a)   ♠ K 9 3   b)   ♠ K Q 3
      ♡ 8   ♡ A 7 4
      ◇ A K Q 7 4 2   ◇ –
      ♣ J 10 7   ♣ A J 10 7 5 4 2

On (a) respond to 1 NT with 3 NT — never mind the singleton heart. On (b) you can respond 3♣, as you are definitely interested in a club slam if opener can help to fill the gaps in your long suit.

11 Intervening bids — the 'Telling' Bids

As you may have noticed, in many other books and in most news-paper articles, South is always the declarer. At one of the bridge courses we ran we found a dear lady who, sitting West, passed on a massive hand because South had opened, and she didn't realise that she wasn't only there to make up the number at the table.

We've told you there is a lot to learn about bridge and that you can't learn it all at once, and so far we have let you take it easy with-out interference from the opposition. In real life many auctions are strongly contested. But remember that both partnerships should be trying to help each other. You will get great pleasure out of this game, learning to bid correctly, to play correctly, to make your contract, or to defeat the enemy contract. The pleasure of defending a contract and being able to defeat it because you and your partner are on the same wavelength with leads and defen-sive signals comes a little later in the course, but now let's think of the times when you will be able to steal the contract away from the opening bidder, or even find a 'save', where you lose only a few points in exchange for preventing your opponents from scoring a game.

It is impossible to lay down precise guide lines for making inter-vening bids, or overcalls, when the bidding has been opened by the other side. It's one of the sections where you will have to use your own judgement, but if we try to explain some of the situations you will come across, and why you bid one thing instead of another, you will find that we shall do away with the occasions on which you will have to guess, and your judgement will be limited only to whether you are an optimist or a coward.

Let's make one thing clear from the start. The *opening* bidder is the one who should have his correct values, but there are many hands on which you would not open but on which you *would* intervene, particularly at the one-level where very little harm can come to you.

There are four main reasons for intervening — get these into your heads once and for all and if your hand doesn't conform to any of them, then learn that most difficult of all bids, 'No Bid'.

Reasons for Intervening, or Overcalling:
1) To discover whether you and your partner hold enough strength to gain the contract for yourselves.
2) To suggest a good lead — a line of attack — if you and your partner become the defenders.
3) To make some effort at opposition which may result in your opponents bidding too high and failing in their contract rather than making it.
4) To prepare the way for a possible 'sacrifice' (generally when your opponents are vulnerable and you are not).

As a prospective intervening bidder, unless you have enough strength to be pretty sure of gaining the contract for your side, be careful of the quality of the suit you bid. Probably because your partner will think you have tops in the suit he will lead it if you become the defenders, and if you have bid it on peanuts, valuable time for you and your partner to get together in the defence will have been lost.

Earlier in this lesson we said that it was difficult to lay down precise guidelines for intervening bids, but now we are going to try to take your problems away from you. Let's look at some of the positions simply and clearly, and explain how you and your partner should never be completely lost and in the dark. It's all a bit difficult, so grip the edge of the table, but we shall take it gradually and, believe us, suddenly the whole thing will become clear.

Simple Intervening Bids in a New Suit: First, let's deal with the occasions on which you are sitting in the West seat, that is, with South the opening bidder on your right. You are the next to bid and hold something like this:

a) ♠ A Q 6 4 2   b) ♠ K 8 2   c) ♠ A K Q 6
   ♡ K J 7   ♡ A 10 9 7 3   ♡ 4 3 2
   ◇ 7 5 2   ◇ 4 3 2   ◇ 4 3 2
   ♣ 5 3   ♣ 3 2   ♣ K Q 8

The first thing to think about is whether or not you are vulnerable, which means that if you get doubled the penalties can be higher than the contract is worth. You know the hand on your right has points, but the one on your left is an unknown quantity. If the balance of the points lie there you will be doubled and caught like the jam in the sandwich. On hand (a) you can bid 1♠ over an opening 1♣, 1◇ or 1♡. Even if you run into trouble, the opponents probably have a game on, and remember that, particularly with an overcall in spades, you make it impossible for your left-hand opponent to bid at the one-level, as he well might wish to do.

On hand (b) it would be worth bidding 1♡ over 1♣ or 1◇, but only if not vulnerable, and it would *not* be worth an intervening bid of 2♡ over 1♠ which could cost you a packet if doubled on your left.

Remember that such bids are not just intended for their nuisance value against your opponents, but to have positive results.

Firstly, as we've already said, you may make it difficult for your left-hand opponent to make a 'free' bid, and secondly you alert your partner at an early stage that you have a suit with some values in it. Your partner could well have more than his share of values — that is, of the missing points — and might be able to support you.

Learners should make it a golden rule never to overcall on less than a 5-card suit. Not only have you something to play with, but partner can raise on a 3-card fit. But with only four trumps, what are you to do if you are doubled? (c) above is the only exception, as a bid of 1♠ would at least indicate a good lead, and to pop in a bid at the 1-level, even if it gets doubled, on such a good 4-card suit, can often do more good than harm.

You will notice that we have mentioned stopping your left-hand opponent from making a free bid. Let's take a moment to explain this more fully. He has heard his partner open 1♣, 1◇, or even 1♡. He could well have a hand on which he would have wanted to bid 1◇ opposite 1♣, or perhaps 1♡ opposite 1♣ or 1◇, or he could even have a hand containing up to 9 points on which he would have liked to bid 1 NT. Suddenly, if you intervene with 1♠, he is fixed unless he has a hand which in any case was good enough to bid at the 2-level. Now he can only bid 1 NT if he has a spade guard.

Let's make another thing clear. If it's your partner who has opened the bidding, you do *not* have to stretcn your hand to find a bid if there has been an intervening bid, which can also apply to

S	W	N	E
1◇	1♠	2◇	?

the fourth player at the table. East has heard the other three players at the table bidding. He knows his partner has made only a simple overcall and may not have the full values for an opening bid, so he's not forced to compete in the auction unless holding positive values.

Finally, before we go on to strong and forcing intervening bids, a word of warning. If you make a simple overcall at the 2-level, check carefully on the texture of your suit. For example, if the suit you want to bid is K-J-9-7-5-3, and you have no entry to your dummy if you become declarer and you have to play this suit from your own hand, you could well lose more tricks in it than might appear at first glance. If the suit lies badly, every time you play either a high or a low card, it could be won by an opponent with a slightly higher card. It is much safer if you have a sequence, so that, playing from the top, you can force out the opponents' high cards and still keep control. The sort of suit we mean is Q-J-10-x-x-x or J-10-9-8-x-x. After you have knocked out the high cards you should be able to draw the opponents' trumps or, as we sometimes call them, their teeth.

After that little digression, let's go back to overcalls.

Jump Intervening Bid: Please notice that for the moment we are dealing with hands on which you want to *tell* your partner the suit in which you want to play. We shall come to the ones on which you want to *ask* him later, but for the moment let's suppose you have a hand with good full values for an opening bid as well as a good suit of your own.

a) ♠ A K J 10 6 5   b) ♠ 3 2   c) ♠ K Q 10 9 8 7 3 2
   ♡ A J 10   ♡ A Q J 10 9 7   ♡ 4 3
   ◇ 6 4   ◇ K 7 4   ◇ 8
   ♣ 7 5   ♣ A 5   ♣ 7 6

On hand (a) if your right-hand opponent opens 1♣, 1◇ or 1♡, bid 2♠. Don't leave partner wallowing in the belief that you hold *only* a simple overcall such as we saw on p. 68. On hand (b) over-call 1♣ or 1◇ with 2♡, or 1♠ with 3♡. These jumps are *not* forc-ing, which means that partner is free to pass, but he will know that you have a good hand plus a 6-card suit, and will give you support if he himself has some values.

Hand (c) is a very different matter. You have not got the values for a straightforward opening bid, but if you bid 3♠ (a jump of one extra level) over a one-level opening bid in any other suit on your right you will not only tell partner that you have a very long suit with no defensive values, and that spades is the suit in which you want to play, but you may well have made life very difficult for your opponents, in addition to warning partner that you would need a great deal of strength from him if you are to have a try for game for your side, though he may well be able to judge that this is going to be one of those 'sacrifice' occasions where you could bid on in spades rather than let the opposition score a game.

Still on the theme of *telling* partner rather than *asking* him, we come now to another important bid and that is . . .

The 1 NT Intervening Bid: Before going further, let's try to stop you making the mistake which many players, even experienced ones, fall into. You must remember that with overcalls and defen-sive bidding you are trying to get a bargain. Your first aim is to get a plus score for your side, and your second not to score too big a minus. Just stop to think whether any action you take can lead you into trouble or, perhaps, whether the opposition will just be warned that they must stop bidding before *they* get into trouble. Take this hand, for example.

♠ J 8 3
♡ K J 10 5
◇ K Q 6 4
♣ A 8

You have 14 points, maximum for an opening weak (12-14 point) No Trump, but if the player on your right bids 1◇ or 1♡, why hurry to his rescue? Bide your time — your hand is worth much more in defence than in attack if your partner should become declarer. One of the biggest traps players fall into is to fail to resist the temptation to bid 1 NT over the opening bid if holding a reasonable hand with something in the opponents' suit. Please let's keep this bid for one type of hand, and one only. Whatever strength of opening No Trump you are using, 1 NT as an overcall should be kept for hands of 16-18 points with, most important of all, a double stopper, or guard, in the opponents' suit. The reason for this is very simple — if you become declarer, the defence has been tipped off as to which suit to attack in.

♠ A J 6
♡ A 10 9
◇ K Q 7 6
♣ K 3 2

♠ K Q 5 2
♡ 7 6
◇ J 10 9 2
♣ A 6 4

Suppose you hold the West hand and, over an opening 1♡ by South, bid 1 NT. Your partner, with the East hand, will raise to 3 NT. You have ten top tricks *if* you can knock out the ◇A. But pause for a moment. After the 1♡ opening the player on your left is going to lead a heart. Your ♡A 10 9 may look attractive to you, but if opener has no more than five hearts and the ◇A, he will make four hearts plus the ◇A and you will give your opponents a plus score — it's even possible that opener has more than five hearts and you will go even more down.

So keep your No-Trump interventions for hands on which you really can cope with the suit opened, even when you know it is going to be led, and that means that you must have a double guard in it, one which will hold the early attack and one which will also hold the further attack when you start on the diamonds. On the West hand above it would be better to double the 1♡ opening — don't worry about it now as we shall be coming to it in detail in the next lesson. Just learn not to bid 1 NT on it, in spite of its 17 points. Exchange the ♡10 and the ◇Q, and now you have a double stop, and can bid 1 NT regardless.

This business of what constitutes a double guard, or stop, in the opponents' suit is very important. In the example above let's give you ♡A-J-8 in the suit opened against you, and in the bad old days this would have been a double guard. Turn back to Lesson 9 and refresh your memories about the correct card to lead if you hold three to an honour of partner's bid suit. If you're still in the dark ages of leading, say, the queen from Q-x-x (top of partner's bid suit!) that ♡ A-J-8 becomes a perfectly good double stop. But it *isn't* if you get a low lead. We'll say it's low from ♡Q-9-x. so the ♡K goes up, and whether declarer takes it or decides to duck, one stop is all he's got, now or later, because ultimately the lead will come back *through* him to the honour on his left.

So please remember, for all practical purposes, a 1 NT overcall, or intervening bid, guarantees strength plus a double guard in opener's suit.

Cue Bid of Opponent's Suit: There is one other type of hand to cover in this lesson, and that is on the rare occasions when you pick up a rock-crusher and to your disgust hear the hand on your right open the bidding.

So far you've learned about three types of overcall, a simple bid at the lowest available level, a jump bid in your own suit, strong but not forcing, and a 1 NT overcall, guaranteeing 16-18 points and a double stop in the opponent's suit. Now you must learn to tell your partner about that rock-crusher. Suppose you hold one of these three hands:

a) ♠ A K Q 10 8 6 2   b) ♠ A K Q J 4   c) ♠ A K
   ♡ 7   ♡ —   ♡ K 4
   ◇ A 8   ◇ K Q 9 3   ◇ A Q J 9 7 6
   ♣ K Q 3   ♣ A J 10 7   ♣ A 8 3

With each of these hands when your right hand opponent opens 1♡ you need so very little from your partner to score a game that you must be able to give him the message, and this you do by way of what is called a cue bid, that is, by bidding two of your opponent's suit. This doesn't mean you've got strength in it — in (b) you've even got a void — but it does mean that partner will know you have a terrific hand and that little or nothing in his will be all you need. He will keep the bidding open for you by bidding his own best suit, after which you will show him yours, and by easy stages, because partner will honour his obligation not to pass until game is reached, you will reach your best final contract.

There are other bids in this overcalling position which we shall be coming to in a later lesson. Meanwhile if we overload your minds with too much that is new, you will forget it all. So for this lesson, just learn, mark, read, and inwardly digest the fact that any particular overcall denies the right type of hand to make another. If you call 1♠ over 1♡, you couldn't call 2♠ or 1 NT, and your partner must learn to recognise this and, conversely, if you do bid 1 NT, to translate it into terms of what you have; or if you make the jump bid, for example, to realise that you have better than a simple overcall, and so on.

12 Intervening bids — the 'asking' bids

The take-out double — when you have doubled — after partner has replied to your double — double then bid — partner's valuation —two final warnings

You will have noticed that, so far, we have dealt only with the hands on which, though you want to intervene over your right-hand opponent's opening bid, you want to *tell* partner about your best suit and what type of hand you have. Now we are coming to those on which you want to *ask* your partner which of his suits matches yours. Let us, then, introduce you to a new word as an active bid, a bid which makes partner come to life, and that is a double of the opening bid on your right. This is *not* a double for penalties, but an 'asking' bid — asking your partner to tell you which suit he has got.

The type of hand on which you will need to use this asking bid is one which occurs very frequently. Your right-hand opponent opens the bidding and you hold high-card points but no good long suit to show. But if you can discover which suit your partner has got, with your combined holdings you could well make a part-score or even a game. You have, perhaps, four heart and four spades, and to make a blind guess as to which to bid could well be disastrous. If you close your eyes and bid hearts, partner might have spades, and equally, if you bid spades, partner might have hearts. The solution to this problem is to double — a very important bid to add to your growing store of knowledge. You don't risk bidding too high in the auction, so cut out the danger of giving away a penalty. Remember that this double is *not* for penalties unless your partner has already made a positive bid. Let's look at some examples:

a) ♠ A J 6 2 b) ♠ K Q 7 5 c) ♠ 6 2   d) ♠ A Q 6
    ♡ A J 7 3   ♡ Q J 8 6   ♡ A Q 10 6   ♡ Q 8 6 3
    ♢ A J 8 4   ♢ 7   ♢ K J 9 3   ♢ Q 10 7 2
    ♣ 6   ♣ A J 6 2   ♣ A J 4   ♣ K 6

On hand (a), who are you to judge which suit will fit your partner's hand best when dealer on your right opens 1♣? *Ask* your
partner by doubling. The same applies on hand (b) when the opening bid is 1♢ — double to *ask* partner for his suit. On hand (c) you
have 15 points and can well afford to double 1♠ to ask partner for
his suit, which he must show at the 2-level. Hand (d) is still worth a
double of 1♣. Your ♣K is 'working' and if partner bids 1♠ and
is allowed to play there, you are unlikely to come to much
harm.

When you have doubled: Before going on, just a few words of
explanation. If your left-hand opponent makes a bid, your partner doesn't have to reply to your question about his suits unless he
has the values to make a 'free' bid. But if the next hand passes,
partner *must* answer your question even if he has zero points, by
bidding his longest suit. If he has two suits of equal length, he
should bid the lower-ranking of the two unless one is a suit he can
bid at the one-level. For example, if you double an opening 1♡
and your partner has four spades and four clubs, he should
choose 1♠ rather than 2♣. Also he should always show a 4-card
major rather than a 5-card minor if he can do so at a low level.

The immediate question you will be thinking of, if you have a
singleton or even a doubleton of the suit you are doubling, is: Isn't
my partner likely to have length in that suit and no other long
suit? Of course this can happen, and often does, but there are still
no real problems and the situation is quite simple. If partner has
four or five cards in the opponent's suit without an honour, say 9-
7-5-3-2, he bids the nearest 3-card suit he can. You could well be in
a 4-3 trump fit (only seven trumps between you) but you are
unlikely to get doubled for penalties at such a low level, and once
again, if you do go down, the opposition would most likely make
a plus score on the hand anyway.

Secondly, if your partner has an honour as well as length in the
opponent's suit, he can bid 1 NT, telling you that he has no interest in any of your suits.

Lastly it is possible, though it doesn't happen very often, that your partner can convert your 'asking' double into a 'penalty' double by passing, but this will only be if his holding in the opponent's suit is very good. To convert the double to a penalty one at the one-level, your side has to make seven tricks. By doubling you show probably three defensive tricks, so your partner must hold not only very good trump length, but honour cards in it as well, which should amount to at least four defensive tricks. If these tricks are not in the trump suit, your side can probably score more by playing the contract yourselves in either a suit or No Trumps, rather than take a miserable one-trick penalty.

After Partner has replied to your 'asking' double: The actions you can take yourself after *asking* partner for his best suit and getting his reply have certain guide lines. We shall deal with how partner can show strength over your double in a moment, but first let's consider your hand. Remember — this is very important — that you have *made* your partner bid, perhaps on no points at all. If you check back to the four hands given as examples of suitable doubling hands you will see that they contain 13-15 points. So before you can think of going anywhere, you will have to find partner holding 9-11 points or a long suit. Although you have lovely finesses in your suits your partner, as declarer, will have to play from his hand towards dummy for these to succeed, and for this he will have to be able to get back into his own hand. He could well be forced to play at least one of your suits from the table. Supposing, however, we top up the number of honour points you hold — remember, still no long suit so you still want to know what partner's suit is, without guessing which to bid yourself.

	a)	b)	c)
♠	A K 10 8	K Q 7 2	K Q 5 3
♡	A Q J 7	K Q J 6	6 2
♢	Q J 10 8	8	A K 3
♣	6	A K 6 5	A Q 6 4

On (a) if you double 1♣, whichever suit partner bids you can raise to the 2-level, and the same applies on (b) and (c) if you are doubling the suit of which you hold a singleton. But give no more than a single raise because the hand opposite to you may be very bad, so you're not going to get to the 10 or 11 trick level.

If you remember only to give partner a raise when you have these bigger point counts, he will be able to value or revalue his

hand accordingly. Take hand (a), for example. If partner holds
♠9 6 3 2: ♡8 5 4: ◇9 3 2: ♣Q 5 2, he will make eight tricks. But if
partner has a hand such as ♠Q 6 3 2: ♡8 5 4: ◇K 3 2: ♣Q 5 2 your
bid of 2♠ should invite him to go on. *He* will know that *you* know
he may have virtually nothing, which isn't true in the context of
the strength shown.

Double Then Bid: Whilst on the subject of these 'asking' doubles,
there is another use to which they can be put, another gap to fill to
give your partner information and a fuller picture of your hand.
You may find this a little difficult, so grip the edge of the table
again, but it is on the same theme, so this is the right time to learn
it.

You have a stronger hand than those we have already shown
you, not, this time, enough to bid game on your own but one on
which you need very little help from partner to fill your gaps. Nor
are they quite as good as the rock-crushers we showed you in Lesson 11. For example:

a) ♠ A K J 10 6 4   b) ♠ 3
   ♡ A Q J   ♡ A Q J 10 9 7 2
   ◇ K Q 7   ◇ K Q J
   ♣ 8   ♣ A 5

On both these hands you are too good to overcall an opening
1♣ with two of your strong major, or to bid 3♡ over 1♠ on (b),
yet you are not quite strong enough to make a cue bid of opponent's suit (see p. 72). But if you double your opponent's bid first
and then, when your partner shows his suit, as he will do thinking
this is an 'asking' double, you now bid your own suit, you give
partner a simple message, 'Yes, partner, I know I doubled to ask
for your suit, but now I'm telling you I have one of my own.
Nearly game in my own hand, and I only need a little help from
you to bid it.' On hand (a) all partner needs to hold is the ♠Q and
the ◇J, or even the ♡K to make your game very probable. On
hand (b) the ♡K or the ♣K would be enough.

This take-out double can also usefully be used on a strong two-
suiter. Partner is almost sure to reply in the suit you have not got,
but when you rebid he must get the picture that his suit didn't hit
the jackpot and that you hold, in fact, the other two suits.

Finally, don't make an 'asking' double on unbalanced hands
which are not good enough for the treatment just described. One

of the unfortunate things that usually befalls you in bridge is that partner nearly always bids the one suit you don't want to hear. This is not surprising really — the less you have in a suit, the more likely your partner is to have length in it.

> ♠ A 4
> ♡ K Q 10 8 3
> ◇ K J 10 6
> ♣ K 5

So if you have a hand such as this, a 16-pointer, bid your hearts over 1♣. If you double you say to partner, 'Bid your suit as I have some of all the other suits,' but where do you go if partner bids 2♠, 3♠, or even 4♠? And if you carry on over a simple spade bid from him, you will be showing him that you hold the near-rock-crusher type we've explained on the previous page, after which it will be only your own fault if he revalues his hand in the light of what you have said, and puts you to a game you can't possibly make.

Partner's Valuation: From all we have said it should be apparent that when you double your partner has responsibilities. You know he may well have little or nothing, in which case he will make the simplest and lowest-level bid he can. As a corollary to this, if he really has something, it is up to him to tell you you have

> | S | W | N | E |
> |------|-----|----|-----|
> | 1♡ | Dbl | No | 1♠ |

struck oil. In an auction such as this East has promised you little or nothing except that he has, probably, a 4-card spade suit. In

> | S | W | N | E |
> |------|-----|----|-----|
> | 1♡ | Dbl | No | 2♠ |

this second auction, his 2♠ bid is merely telling you that he has a real spade suit and some values. You may pass on a weak double or take the hint and carry on. If he had a really up-and-coming hand he would tell you so by making a cue-bid of the opponent's

> | S | W | N | E |
> |------|-----|----|-----|
> | 1♡ | Dbl | No | 2♡ |

suit. His 2♡ bid doesn't show he holds hearts but passes the buck back to you to choose the suit. It says, in fact, that he has values and is prepared to go along with anything.

Two Final Words of Warning: Firstly a word of warning which we hope has already got through to you. If South has opened the bidding and you, sitting West, have a good holding in his suit, you must *not* double. Remember that the double is an asking bid, asking partner to take out into his own best suit. This is the last thing

♠ K J 3
♡ K J 10 8 7
♢ K 9 2
♣ 7 6

you want if the player on your right has opened 1 ♡ ! It's so logical, isn't it? Bide your time by passing. If your partner should be able to bid a suit of his own, then you have an ample heart stop to prod him into a No-Trump contract. If your partner can't bid there's always a good chance that your opponents will end up playing in a heart contract they can't possibly make (and which you may be able to double later for penalties). Alternatively, it is always possible that after your pass, your left-hand opponent may also pass, and if your partner should make a take-out double, that really would be all this and heaven too!

The second word of warning is that you must *not* double an opening 1 NT if you want partner to take out into a suit. A double of a No Trump opening bid is intended primarily for penalties, and your partner will not take out or, indeed, take any action at all, unless he sees a safer or brighter future for your side. This doesn't mean that you can never take action over a No Trump opening and, in fact, we shall be giving you a whole lesson on what you can do towards the end of this course.

13 Tricks out of thin air

Think at trick 1 — count your tricks — plan at trick 1 — coping with losers before it is too late

In Lesson 7 we warned you to think at trick 1 — to look before you leap into play. It's worth repeating that your opponents will be delighted if you rush into play the moment dummy goes down and then find, later in the hand, that you've missed the only way to make your contract. Some hands are cast iron, that is, you couldn't make a mistake if you tried (though believe us, sometimes learners try!), but on many more occasions success will depend on taking time to study the dummy in relation to your own hand and *counting* your tricks. If you can see for certain that you can make your contract, then get on with it, though no one will blame you for pausing to think out the best way to play the hand, firstly to make certain you can't put your foot in it anywhere, and secondly to see whether you might perhaps make some valuable overtricks, all of which count in the final reckoning.

Let's take a very ordinary situation. Here you have become South, declarer in 4♠, perhaps via the bidding 1♠-2♠-4♠, which is not unreasonable as you have 18 points and know that North is giving you 6 - 9 points and four trumps. West leads the ♡A and you take stock. You have five top spades, three diamond tricks, and the ♣A — one short of your contract. By now either East or West will be showing signs of impatience — 'Get on with it, you can't help losing the hearts!' But in that little pause *you* have thought of a way to manufacture your tenth trick.

♠ 9 7 4 2
♡ 8 7 6 2
◇ A Q 7 3
♣ 6

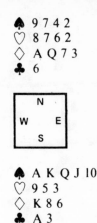

♠ A K Q J 10
♡ 9 5 3
◇ K 8 6
♣ A 3

West presses on with top hearts and you lose the first three tricks — all you can afford. He leads a fourth winning heart (East has long since run out of hearts and has discarded small clubs) and you ruff in your own hand. Now you set out to draw trumps and find, rather to your disgust, that West never had a spade, so East has four. If you draw all his trumps you will have none left either in your own hand or dummy, and unless you are lucky and find the diamonds 3-3, you will be left with a losing club because you will have nowhere to park it. So *lay off* drawing trumps whilst you still have some in dummy. Play your ♣ A and ruff a club in dummy for your tenth trick. But use the ♠ 9 on the principle that you never send a boy on a man's errand, and East may have got rid of his clubs so that he might over-ruff a smaller trump. Now draw the rest of the trumps and play your winning diamonds. It doesn't matter if they break or not because you have got rid of your losing club.

Now let's give each hand one less heart and one more club. West leads the ♡ A which you know heralds the coming of the ♡ K on the next trick. As we hope you have learned to do by now, you stop and take stock. You can count five top spades, three top diamonds, and the ♣ A, again one short of your contract. Again the trumps may or may not break well — the possibilities are 4-0, 3-1 or 2-2, and the diamonds may break 3-3 but you don't want to rely on that. Have you made your plan? Well, today you're going to learn that most difficult of all lessons for beginners, deliberately to lose a trick!

You ruff the third heart in your own hand. You are down to

♠ 9 7 4 2
♡ 8 7 6
◇ A Q 7 3
♣ 6 4

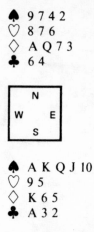

♠ A K Q J 10
♡ 9 5
◇ K 6 5
♣ A 3 2

four trumps now, but you can afford to test the suit as it is always
nice to have the opponents' teeth out of the way if you can afford
it. Once again, you find to your disappointment that West has
none and East four. But there's nothing to worry about as long as
you have counted your tricks and keep your head. Once again lay
off drawing trumps and cash the ♣A. Now — wait for it! — play a
small club from either hand. These were losers from now till
Christmas, as even if the diamonds oblige by breaking 3-3 you will
only be able to get rid of one club from your own hand. It's true
that the diamond break would enable you to make ten tricks for
your contract, but do you want to rely on that when you can make
it for certain? Of course you don't (and when this hand was dealt
in real play, East held ◇ J-10-x-x). Now that you have lost the
club trick, what harm can the opponents do to you? Let's assume
that East wins, and guessing what you are up to, tries to frustrate
you by returning a trump. You win in hand, lead your third small
club, and ruff it with the ♠9. You still have a trump in dummy to
lead back to your own hand — even if you hadn't, you could get
back via the ◇K. Now you draw the remaining trumps, take your
top diamonds and make ten tricks, whereas without thought you
could have lost two hearts, and as many as two clubs if you'd had
to use all four of dummy's trumps in the process of drawing East's
before you did something more constructive.

Now we'll change the set-up again, even changing the suits so
that you don't get the idea that spades are always trumps and that
it's always losing clubs you have to cope with. Here you are
South, declarer in 4♡. It's a little difficult to imagine how you got

♠ 8 6 4 3 2
♡ J 10 7
◇ Q
♣ A J 6 4

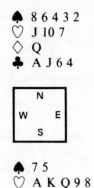

♠ 7 5
♡ A K Q 9 8
◇ 8 2
♣ K Q 7 5

there, so let's just say it was an unfortunate bidding misunderstanding and entirely your partner's fault.

This time West leads the ♠A and what does your stock-taking reveal? Five trump tricks and four clubs, with no possibility of a discard anywhere. The trumps can't break better than 3-2, so if you don't make a constructive plan before you draw the opponents' teeth you will have *none* left in dummy, and will find yourself left at the end with two losers in spades and two in diamonds.

This is a little harder than the previous examples, but can you work it out assuming that West continues with his second top spade at trick 2, East shows out, and West then plays a third top spade? Yes, it's that diamond position, isn't it?

You ruff the third spade and *play a small diamond.* You are pretty confident that East will win this trick because West has already shown up with five honours in spades, and if he'd had a top diamond honour he would surely have bid 1♠ over your opening 1♡. The reason you're glad about this is that you don't want another spade shot at you by West to shorten your trumps to three.

You are right — East wins the diamond and, knowing what you plan to do, returns a trump. No other return would help him more than this. You win in your own hand, lead your second lowly diamond, ruff it in dummy, lead the last trump back to your own hand and draw the remaining trumps, after which you cash your four winning clubs and you're home and dry.

Declarer plays of this sort come in all shapes and sizes. Sometimes you can win the original lead but have your losers, too many of them, in other places. Whatever the actual set-up, making your contract is going to depend on coping with losers before you lose the ability to do so. Sometimes you can ruff out, or establish, side suits for discards, as we did in Lesson 6, but constantly you'll go down when you needn't because you didn't remember to look before you leaped at Trick 1. 'Sorry, partner, there was nothing I could do about it!' But was there something you could have done? Here's another example.

♠ 7
♡ 7 5 3
◇ A K 8 7 5
♣ 7 6 5 4

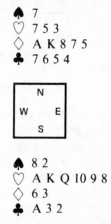

♠ 8 2
♡ A K Q 10 9 8
◇ 6 3
♣ A 3 2

This time you're playing in 4♡ against which West leads the ♣ K. Even though you can win the first trick without trouble, you need just as much time to think and plan as you did before. You can see a certain spade loser, two club losers, and a second spade loser if you don't do something about it. You can't plan, as we did in Lesson 6, to cope by establishing dummy's diamonds for discards, as you are short of entries, but there is a very simple way out of it. Win the opening and play a small spade from either hand. The worst the defence can do is take their two established club winners, after which no switch will hurt you. You will win the next trick whatever they lead, play your last spade and ruff in dummy, and then draw trumps and claim the rest.

Here's a final example which is really on exactly the same theme, but it is designed to show you that other factors can come into your line of play, and sometimes even more courage than we have required of you so far is needed to make your contract. You are South, declarer in 6♠ against which West leads the ◇ K. As they say in the bridge quizzes, plan your play.

You have a certain diamond loser, and if the club finesse is

♠ J 10 9 4
♡ A 7 6 5
♢ 8 6
♣ A Q 8

♠ A K Q 8 3
♡ K 8
♢ A 7 2
♣ J 10 7

wrong you will have to add a club loser, which is one too many.
You will, therefore, have to play for the club finesse to be right,
but you've got to do something about your third diamond, as you
have no way of getting rid of it by discarding. The answer, which
will be obvious to you by now, is to ruff it while the going is good.
In at trick 1 with the ♢A, you test the trumps. If both opponents
follow, you draw them, because you will still have the one vital
trump in dummy. If one opponent turns out to have all four missing ones, then you must stop drawing trumps and, agony of agon-
ies in a slam contract, deliberately lose a trick by playing a losing
diamond from both hands.

But now, provided the club finesse comes off, you're home and
dry. Win any return in hand, lead your last diamond and ruff,
draw the rest of the trumps and take the club finesse by leading the
♣J from hand.

We shall be looking at some more advanced play techniques
later in this course, but this should be enough for now.

14 Covering Honours

When to cover — when not to cover

This is your second lesson as a defender, and it is important for you to learn when to play a high card and when not to. Many of you will have heard the so-called golden rules, 'second hand plays low' and 'third hand plays high', but rules, even golden ones, were made to be broken, so please add to these two 'unless you have good reason not to'.

What we are talking about now is the question of covering an honour with an honour, and you will get the idea more easily if you remember that covering — that is, playing an honour when declarer leads an honour, from either his own hand or dummy — is designed to make him use up two of his honours if he wants the trick, and possibly to 'promote' a winner for your side. Let's look at a very simple example.

Q 7 5

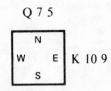

K 10 9

Declarer crosses to dummy (or perhaps he's already in dummy) and leads the queen. You can assume that he's doing this because he has a holding headed by the A-J. If you *don't* cover the queen with your king, his queen will win the trick and he will then lead a small one from dummy and finesse by playing the knave from his own hand. He will then cash the ace for three tricks in the suit. If, on the other hand, you play your king on his queen (second hand playing high!), he will have to use up his ace to win the trick. It's true that his knave will then become a winner for the second round of the suit, but your ten will have been *promoted* to winning rank for the third round.

Q 7 5

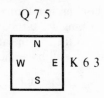

K 6 3

Now let's see what difference it would make if you hadn't got that ten to promote. Would you cover this time? Yes, most certainly you would, because you have to allow for the fact that your *partner* may hold the ten! If you don't cover, declarer will certainly win three tricks in the suit. If you do cover he *may* still win three tricks, but only if he, and not your partner, has the ten.

J 7 5

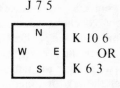

K 10 6
OR
K 6 3

Would you feel hard done by if asked to spare your king to put on the knave in either of these situations? No, you wouldn't. In the first you would realize that declarer held a combination headed by the A-Q so that your ten would be promoted to winning rank for the third round, and in the second you would hope that partner had the ten. You wouldn't cost your side a trick either way by putting up the king, but it might well cost you a trick if you didn't. You would even cover if dummy's high card led through you were no better than the the ten.

Now let's tackle a 'don't' and that is, don't cover if you can see a sequence of touching honours in dummy.

Q J 10 9

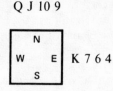

K 7 6 4

It's not very difficult to see that to cover the queen with your king wouldn't gain either you or your partner anything. There just isn't any chance of promoting anything for your side. It's even possible that declarer's holding is no longer than A-x-x, so that by refusing to cover, your king will ultimately become a winner, and declarer will have to ruff the fourth card if he plays it later from dummy, because you will still have the king to put on it.

Q J 9 8

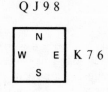

K 7 6

A rule to remember is never to cover the *first* of touching honours. There are two possibilities — declarer, in difficulty for entries, has led the queen and your partner holds the singleton ace, in which case your king and his ace would crash together; or, in the diagram shown, declarer has the ace. If you cover the first time, that is put on your king when he leads the queen from dummy, he will win with the ace, and is now in a position to finesse against your partner for the ten. So hold back, if you can, until you can cover the *last* of touching honours. Look at this example carefully. If declarer leads the queen from dummy, play your six. If he follows with the knave, *now* cover, because the finesse position will have been killed.

There are two more important 'don'ts' before we go on to look at other situations. Firstly, don't ever cover if you know that the opponents are long in the suit. A typical example would be if declarer had made a bid showing length in his suit and you know he must have at least six. When dummy goes down you see Q-x-x-x, so now, if you think for a moment, you will realize that, if you have two, your partner can't have more than a singleton. You, holding K-x, might thoughtlessly cover the queen with your king and, horror of horrors, crash your partner's singleton ace! In the same way, if dummy's knave is led when you know about length, and you have the K-x, don't cover, because partner's singleton might be the queen. If partner hasn't got the queen, nothing will have been lost by holding back, because your king was going to lose on a finesse anyway.

Finally, *don't wriggle* or hesitate when faced with a decision whether or not to cover. When you see a possible covering situation looming up when dummy goes down, you, just as much as declarer, have the right to think at trick 1. You must never make it seem that you are wondering what to play on the first trick if you know what you're going to do. Take the card you intend to play out of your hand and put it face down on the table. Then just say that that's the card you are going to play, but you're thinking about the rest of your defence. *Don't* leave any 'think' about covering until it's right on you, because then all you will be doing is as good as saying you've got the card declarer is worrying about. So play smoothly, particularly if you have decided not to cover, so that you don't give anything away. Once you've wriggled and hesitated, you might as well cover and be done with it.

There is one aspect of covering or not covering where many people slip up and that is when your partner leads a card and dummy goes down with one or more honours. Apply exactly the same

Q 8 4

	N	
6 led	**W** **E**	K 3 2
	S	

rules as we have given you here. If it's a single honour put up by declarer, cover just as you would do if declarer himself had led the queen from the table. In the same way, *don't* cover the first of touching honours when partner leads the suit and declarer plays an honour from the table. It is very far from unknown for declarer to pull a fast one on you in the hope that you will fall for it. Look at the next one: declarer's got the singleton ace which he was going to have to play anyway. If he puts up dummy's queen on your partner's lead and you fall into the trap of covering with your king, all you will have accomplished will be to make the rest of dummy's holding good, leaving declarer no problems about establishing the suit. If you refuse to cover — but do it smoothly so that declarer is left wondering whether you have the king or East

Q J 10 9 5

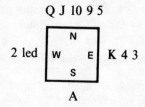

2 led

K 4 3

A

has made a thoroughly bad lead away from an unsupported king — declarer will have to ruff out your king before dummy's suit becomes good.

Now let's turn to the other side of the table, because it isn't always a nice visible holding in dummy that you, as a defender, have to think about. Very often there is an honour 'tenace' (remember the word? — it means broken honour holding) in dummy, and you, sitting on declarer's left, have to decide whether or not to cover the honour he leads. In the previous examples you could see dummy's cards and could make shrewd assumptions about declarer's holdings. Now you can see dummy's holding, and have to make assumptions about what declarer has.

A Q 6

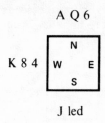

K 8 4

J led

You can take it from us that a good declarer, unless he has entry problems, won't be leading the knave unless he has the ten behind it. His correct play would be to lead low and finesse the queen in the hope that West (you) holds K-x only. But often there are entry problems, so in the situation shown you *should* cover, in the hope either that East, your partner, has the ten, or that East has four headed by the nine, in which case, even though it may be ruffed if you are playing in a suit contract, your partner's nine will be made into the boss boy. If you're playing in No Trumps, *any* fourth card partner holds will become a winner. Even the ♣2, which is supposed to have an inferiority complex because it's the lowest card in the pack, could become a winner in this way.

A 4

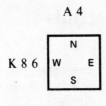

K 8 6

Q led

Here's another very big 'don't'. Although your natural reaction might be to cover declarer's queen with your king, you have nothing to gain by doing so. Whether playing in a trump suit contract or in No Trumps, declarer will have to play the ace on the second round, leaving your king boss of the suit. In other words, don't cover if you know that your honour can't be caught. Let's extend this to one final example:

A 7 4

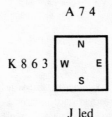

K 8 6 3

J led

If declarer is truly leading from a J-10 combination, your partner's queen will win. If he is trying to fool you by leading the knave when he also has the queen, no good will come from covering because your king can't be caught.

Here's one final word of advice, and that is that you should never cover from pure force of habit. Only do so when there is a concrete chance of promoting a winner for your side. All the other strictures, such as not hesitating or wriggling, apply just as much as they did when you were in the East seat.

15 Opener's Rebids

Obligation to rebid — new suit rebids — supporting partner's suit — No Trump limit rebids — rebids at the 3-level — reverse rebids

In this lesson we are going to concentrate solely on what opener bids at his second chance. For a start you can take it that the opponents have kept silent throughout so you, as opener, have chosen your opening bid, heard a response from your partner, and now you have to bid again.

There is one vitally important rule to learn — and never forget it:

Rebidding by Opener:
  Unless your partner has previously passed, or has made a limit bid in reply to your opening bid, *you must bid again.*

To explain this a little more fully, if, for example, your partner were in a position to bid before the auction got round to you, and his bid were a pass — imagine him North and you South in this bit of the auction — North passed before you got a chance, so if you open the bidding, as you have done here, with 1♡ and he now bids 1♠ you *need* not bid again if you think it wiser to pass. Don't run away with the idea that you *mustn't* bid again — frequently you will want to, but it isn't obligatory.

```
S      W      N      E
              No     No
1♡     No     1♠     No
?
```

Now turn back to Lessons 4 and 6, and revise what you have already learned about responder's limit bids, in both suits and No Trumps. Whether he has passed before you bid or not, these responses will carry exactly the same meanings. They are non-forcing, which means you need not bid again if you think it wisest to pass in the light of what you have been told of partner's strength — or weakness.

That leaves us with a change of suit by responder when he has not previously passed, and this is *unconditionally forcing*. In other words, when you choose an opening bid you must allow for the fact that partner may respond in another suit, so you must, when you open, be prepared to rebid, and what you must aim to do is to clarify your hand. Remember that neither of you should be just sitting there bidding your own cards without reference to your partner. He needs to get a picture of your hand just as much as you need a picture of his.

Rebidding your Original Suit: As you are trying to clarify your hand for your partner, if you make your rebid in your original suit it *must* mean that you have no other suit to show. But here's an easy little rule for you (we've mentioned it before):

A four-card suit is biddable, but it is not rebiddable

Translating this, if you choose to open the bidding, as is perfectly in order, on a suit which contains only four cards, you can't *rebid* it unless partner supports it. In other words, if the auction goes 1♠-2♢-2♠ you have *rebid* your spades, which must mean that you have a minimum of a 5-card suit. A simple rebid at the lowest available level in your opening suit will generally be what we call a sign-off bid, that is, you have nothing more constructive to say.

At this point it would be as well for you to revise Lesson 8 on your choice of opening bid, after which we will run over the examples on the next page.

With hand (a), whether partner responds 1♠, 2♣ or 2♢, you have no possible rebid other than 2♡, a repeat of your suit at the

a) ♠ 9 7 6   b) ♠ A Q 10 8 6 5   c) ♠ A K Q J 10 7
   ♡ A K 10 8 4   ♡ 9 6 3   ♡ A 5
   ◇ Q 8   ◇ A 8   ◇ 9 2
   ♣ K 6 2   ♣ 6 2   ♣ Q 6 4

lowest available level. You have a minimum hand — it adds up to
13 points only because of the fifth heart — so tell your partner you
have nothing further to say and won't bid again unless he forces
you to do so. Hand (b) is exactly the same story except that this
time your suit is spades. Don't boggle because, even with the fifth
and sixth spades, it only adds up to 12 points. It would be foolish
indeed to pass with a suit, particularly spades, which you can bid
and rebid until the cows come home if need be.

Hand (c) is a very different story. This time you are absolutely
certain of being able to make seven tricks as long as you are
allowed to play in spades. Give partner the good news by making
a *jump* rebid of 3♠, showing a 6-card suit. This is not 100% forcing
though it is extremely unlikely that a partner who can respond at
all will allow the auction to drop below game.

New Suit Rebids: Especially if you are not very keen on partner's
suit, you should take your earliest possible chance to show him an
alternative in your own hand if you have one. Once again, here are
some examples:

a) ♠ K Q 9 4 2   b) ♠ 10 4   c) ♠ K Q 9 4 2
   ♡ A J 8 7 3   ♡ A Q 10 7 6   ♡ 9
   ◇ 9   ◇ K J 6 5   ◇ K 7
   ♣ K 7   ♣ K 8   ♣ A J 8 7 3

On hand (a) you will have opened 1♠, the higher-ranking of
equal and adjacent suits. If partner bids 2♣ or 2◇, show your second suit by rebidding 2♡. This is no more forcing than 2♠ would
be, but it gives partner a chance to revalue his hand in the knowledge that you have two suits. Even hand (b) you should treat in
the same way. Open 1♡ and if partner bids 1♠ or 2♣, neither
of which you like very much, rebid 2◇, showing at least a 4-card
diamond suit. On hand (c) you open 1♣ allowing for a red suit
response when you will rebid 1♠.

Supporting Partner's Suit: If you open the bidding and partner
makes a change-of-suit response which you like, it's only common

sense that you should support him. Never be selfish — however good your suit is. Remember that a trump fit is the all-important thing for success in a contract. Once again, examples will explain this best:

a) ♠ K J 8   b) ♠ K Q 8   c) ♠ A K 8
   ♡ 10 8 7 6   ♡ 10 8 7 6   ♡ 10 8 7 6
   ◇ A   ◇ A   ◇ A
   ♣ A J 10 6 5   ♣ A K 10 6 5   ♣ A K 10 6 5

With hand (a) you would open 1♣ and, if partner responded 1◇ or 1♠ you could do nothing but repeat your clubs, showing at least a 5-card suit. If, however, he responded 1♡ your obvious rebid would be 2♡. You have at least a 4-4 heart fit — let him choose, according to his strength, whether to stop there or go on towards game. Hand (b) is the same 'shape' but stronger. If partner is minimum for his response you don't want to force him up too high, but he will have at least four hearts (bidding at the one-level he need not have five) and 6 points upwards. Rebid 3 ♡ and leave him to judge whether to stop there or go on to 4 ♡ . With hand (c) if partner responds to your 1 ♣ with 1 ♡ you don't care how weak his response. Jump direct to 4 ♡ and let him get on with it.

Note, by the way, that your partner must do his bit by 'translating' your rebids. In the last sequence relating to hand (c), if he should be maximum, or near maximum, for his 1♡ bid, it's up to him to take the hint (more than a hint, because you have said that however weak his 1♡ response you are not prepared to play below game) and investigate for a possible slam contract.

No Trump Limit Bid Rebids: You will find there are many hands on which you won't want to rebid your suit weakly, you don't want to show a second suit, and you're not in a position to support partner's, and here the No Trump limit bids can well come into their own.

As always, a limit bid is non-forcing and partner may pass, but he does so at his peril if he fails to correlate the meaning of the bid with his own hand and work out whether or not he should raise. There's one other thing to recap on, and that is that once you've made a limit bid *you will not bid again* unless partner makes a bid which asks you to do so. So the bidding could never go, for instance, as here:

$$1\heartsuit - 1\spadesuit$$
$$2\,NT - 3\spadesuit$$
$$3\,NT$$

2 NT was a limit bid and 3♠ was partner's decision as to the best final contract in the light of the limit bid. Opener *cannot* dredge up a further bid unless he's discovered an extra ace hidden behind his little cards!

The precise values of the No Trump rebids vary according to whether the response has been at the one or the two level. The reason for this, of course, is that a response at the one-level (1◇ - 1♡) might be made on as little as 6 points, whereas a response at the two-level guarantees a minimum of 8 points, so slightly less points in opener's hand are needed to keep within a safety level. When he hears the limit bid, partner (responder) is expected to relate the values shown to his own hand and pass or rebid as common sense dictates.

The following table, which should be learned by heart, is calculated on a reasonably conservative basis. As always, 'fit', not to mention the position of the outstanding cards, will come into the final result, but by and large you won't go far wrong.

After a 1-level Response: (1◇ – 1♠)

      Opener's rebid   1 NT = 15-16 points
                            2 NT = 17-18 points
                            3 NT = 19 points
                            (See below as to quality of points)

After a 2-level Response: (1◇ – 2♣)

      Opener's rebid: 2 NT = 15-16 points
                            3 NT = 17-19 points

                            (Allowance must always be made for the quality of the hand. 17 points may be a 'bad' 17 with isolated honours and low intermediates. A 'good' 17 will include high intermediates.)

After a response of 1 NT to 1♡ *or* 1♠

                            2 NT shows an opening hand of 17-18 points.
                            3 NT shows an opening hand of 19 points.

The best way to get these opener's rebids into your head will be by studying examples. Please try to treat them as a quiz, deciding on what you would rebid before you look at the answers. Please at this stage too get it into your heads that opener and responder, his partner, are two very different people, with different values shown by their bids. In Lesson 4, for example, you learned that to respond 1 NT to partner's opening 1♡, you showed 6-9 points, and that to respond 2 NT showed 10-12 points. Notice that these same No Trump bids, when used as *opener's rebids,* show quite different values. Now here goes, and let's see just how well you have learned your lessons. You are given your opening hand and your partner's response — what would you rebid in each case?

a) ♠ 9 7 6 2
♡ K Q J 8 4
◇ K 7
♣ A 5
1♡ - 2◇
?

or

1♡ - 1♠
?

b) ♠ J 9 8 6
♡ K Q 9 8 4
◇ K 7
♣ A K
1♡ - 2◇
?

or

1♡ - 1♠
?

c) ♠ K J 9 7
♡ K Q J 10 4
◇ 9 2
♣ A K
1♡ - 2◇
?

or

1♡ - 1♠
?

In (a) facing a 2◇ response you would simply repeat your hearts, 2♡, but if partner should respond 1♠ you would raise to 2♠.

In (b) you have an excellent hand and must not mislead responder into thinking it is no better than (a). Facing a 2◇ response — the one suit you want to hear — rebid 2 NT. If, however, partner should respond 1♠, again you must not leave him in the dark. Bid 3♠. On (c) when partner bids 2◇, knowing that his hand must contain at least 8 points, rebid 3 NT. If his response is 1♠ you are unwilling for him to play below game in what must be a 4-4 fit at least. Bid 4♠.

a) ♠ 9 5
♡ A 9 2
◇ K Q 9 8
♣ A Q 8 4
1◇ — 1♠
?

b) ♠ A J 10
♡ 9 4
◇ A Q 9 8
♣ K Q 10 7
1◇ — 1♡
?

c) ♠ K Q 9
♡ A Q J 5
◇ K J 7
♣ Q 10 6
1♡ — 1 NT
?

On (a) (too strong for 1 NT weak), when partner bids 1♠, rebid 1 NT. If he bids any other suit give him a single raise in it. On (b) your rebid facing 1♡ should be 2 NT, showing the added values. Your 'intermediates' are very good, making it a more than 'good' 16 points. Top it up by, say, making one of the hearts into the ♡Q and you should bid a direct 3 NT. On (c) you have 18 points but when partner responds 1 NT he may have as few as 6 points. Bid an invitational 2 NT, asking him to go on to game if he has better than minimum. Make the ◇J into the ◇Q and you want to have a try for game anyway, so bid a direct 3 NT.

Opener's 3-level Rebids and 'Reverse' Rebids: All you need to know at this stage is that such bids (1♡ - 2◇ - 3 ♣, or 1♡ - 2◇ - 2♠) are usually forcing. They will be taught to you much later but for now, when planning your opening and rebid, just think of this, and that you mustn't make a forcing rebid on a weak hand.

We use a cut-off point of 15 points for a weak or moderate opening bid, and if you have 16 or more points, that is, a strong opening, we rebid differently to show it, which you will learn later on.

16 Signals and Discards

The defensive language of Bridge — a 'peter' — a trump peter

As a defender, playing bridge without the use of signals and meaningful discards you are doing little more than playing snap. We haven't tried to tell you about the language of defence before this because, up to now, it has been all you could do to look at your own cards, let alone your partner's. Now we want you to try to think in some positive terms of speaking to your partner by the cards you play.

At bridge you are not allowed to jump on your chair or wave a flag to attract your partner's attention, but there is a very effective language of signals, made with the actual cards you play, to tell your partner what you want. We don't expect you to remember to make your signals all at once, or even to see a signal if your partner makes one, but we can tell you that the first time you make a signal which your partner sees, and thereby defeat declarer's contract, or when *you* see one of partner's signals with the same result, will be a real thrill.

Your first peep at the art of defending a hand came in the lesson on opening leads. As a defender you don't just sit there whilst declarer happily makes his contract — you do your level best to stop him. Now here's your second peep. Defensive signals go a very long way, but we shan't try to thrust more down your throats at this stage than you can swallow. Your very first step, then, is to learn that the play of a high card means either 'Yes, I like it —

carry on with the suit you are playing,' or, alternatively, if you are discarding, the play of a high card means, 'Switch to this suit if you get a chance.' As usual, we'll explain this more fully.

Signals are based on the simple fact that the normal order in which to play your cards is to get rid of the little ones first, so that if you vary this by playing a high card when you could play a low one, you are doing something out of the ordinary *of which you hope partner will take notice.* Let's take a very simple situation first:

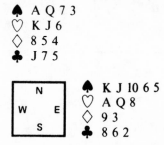

♠ A Q 7 3
♡ K J 6
◇ 8 5 4
♣ J 7 5

♠ K J 10 6 5
♡ A Q 8
◇ 9 3
♣ 8 6 2

Assume that you are defending South's heart contract, against which West, your partner, leads the ♣ A. Do you want him to carry on with this suit? Does it, in fact, seem to you to offer a good line of defence? No, it doesn't. From his lead you expect him to have the ♣ K, and possibly the ♣ Q as well, but you have no interest. You would prefer him to dream up a switch to spades, so play the discouraging little ♣ 2. With any luck he will now try a spade through the 'tenace' on the table, and you will subsequently be able to put him back on lead by returning a second club to lead through spades again.

Suppose, however, that you hold exactly the same hand but this time, against a heart contract, partner leads the ◇ A. You expect him to have the ◇ K too, and if you think for a moment you will realise that South must have a pretty weak hand. If West has 7 points in the ◇ A-K there are only 12 high-card points left for South. He really must have six hearts and the top club honours, but what damage you can do if you get the right defence! Don't blindly play the discouraging ◇ 3, but play the ◇ 9. Surely partner will notice this high card! If he does he will continue with the ◇ K to see if you really mean it, and when on the second round you play the ◇ 3, he will know you did! If only declarer holds three diamonds and your partner can be persuaded to play a third round, you will be able to ruff it with the ♡ 8. That will be three tricks, you sit over dummy's heart honours for two tricks in that suit, and may well make a spade trick. And all because when partner led that ◇A you were able to say, 'Yes, partner, *I like it —* carry on.'

This play of a high card followed by a lower one is known as a 'peter'. It has other names such as 'echo' or 'high-low'. Just know them in case you hear them and wonder what they mean, but we shall use the usual name of 'peter'.

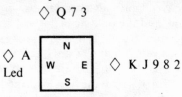

◇ Q 7 3

◇ A
Led

◇ K J 9 8 2

Let's look at another example to make sure you get into your head this terrific new concept of speaking to your partner with cards. Your partner leads the ◇A. Just why you're not sure because you know he hasn't got the ◇K. Probably, then, he has only the ◇ A doubleton, but *you* know that this lead was a splendid idea. Encourage with the ◇9 — not the ◇8 which is the same value. If your guess is right, he will continue with another diamond and you, sitting over the ◇Q, will take the first three tricks in diamonds. If West started with two diamonds, he may be able to tell you on the third round what he would like *you* to lead next.

This brings us to the second concept in petering, and that is when you are discarding because you can't follow suit to whatever declarer is playing — probably he's drawing trumps, or running a long suit in No Trumps.

♠ 6 4
♡ A K 8 3
◇ 8 6 2
♣ 7 6 3 2

This time you are East and can only follow to two rounds of spades, trumps, when declarer is playing to draw them. He plays a third spade and you, desperately wanting a heart to be led if partner wins a trick, play the ♡8. This should be a very clear message to your partner as to what you want him to lead if he gets the chance.

Sometimes you won't have just the right cards in your hand to pass the message clearly. Change the hand you held to this:

♠ 6 4
♡ A K 3 2
◇ 8 6 2
♣ 7 6 3 2

Now you haven't got a high heart to discard to attract your partner's attention, and it would be better to discard either the ◇2 or the ♣2 on the third trump. If it does nothing else it will warn partner that this is a suit you don't want led. If it's clear from the cards in dummy or what has gone before that you couldn't want a diamond lead, then discard the low club and, vice versa, if you couldn't want a club, then warn partner that you don't want a diamond. A partner worth his salt will realise that if you've got *anything*, it must be in hearts.

There is, however, another possibility. Suppose you had only a singleton trump (spade). Then the probability is that, in drawing trumps, declarer will give you the chance to discard twice. If you think this is likely, you can discard the ♡3 followed by the ♡2. It's still a peter, although you had only small cards to do it with — the ♡3 followed by the ♡2 should alert your partner to the fact that you want a heart led.

Before we go on to the last signal we propose to teach you at this stage, let's just look at a complete hand and the devastating effect that partnership co-operation in defence can cause.

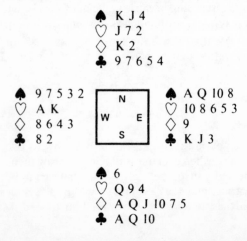

♠ K J 4
♡ J 7 2
◇ K 2
♣ 9 7 6 5 4

♠ 9 7 5 3 2   ♠ A Q 10 8
♡ A K   ♡ 10 8 6 5 3
◇ 8 6 4 3   ◇ 9
♣ 8 2   ♣ K J 3

♠ 6
♡ Q 9 4
◇ A Q J 10 7 5
♣ A Q 10

Diamonds are trumps and West leads the ♡K. Thinking back to your lesson on opening leads, you know that this means that he either has the ♡Q or the ♡A-K bare. However, you are not at this stage interested in hearts and hope for a spade switch, so discourage with the ♡3. West, however, has his own plans. In spite of your low heart, he continues with the ♡A, so now you know he had only a doubleton to start with. Next he switches to a spade and you win over whatever is played from dummy. You return another heart for West to ruff and West will now probably try another spade. Declarer, however, can ruff, but he has only one entry to dummy, the ◇K. He uses this to enable him to take the club finesse, but he can't do it twice. He can draw the rest of the diamonds and cash his ♣A, but he will be forced to concede a club trick to you at the end, so makes only eight tricks in all when, without co-operation between you and West, he could have made nine tricks. It may not seem much to stop one extra trick, but it can in many circumstances make all the difference. 3◇ one down, or 2◇ just made can, when you reach the heights of playing Duplicate Pairs, make the difference between a 'top' and a 'bottom'.

The Trump Peter: This is the last of the defensive signals we propose to teach you this time. There are many more, but if you have the three basic ones in your armoury you will be well on the way to becoming a good defender.

A trump peter, that is, the play of a trump when following suit, followed by a lower trump, says two things — 'I have three trumps plus something I'd like to use the third one for.' In this way a defender is able to signal to his partner that he started with three trumps *and* that, given the chance, he has a positive use for the third, which is inevitably that he can get in a ruff.

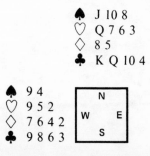

♠ J 10 8
♡ Q 7 6 3
◇ 8 5
♣ K Q 10 4

♠ 9 4
♡ 9 5 2
◇ 7 6 4 2
♣ 9 8 6 3

Defending South's heart contract you, West, lead the ♠9, the suit with which your partner, East, opened the bidding. East wins with the ♠A and returns a second spade which South wins with the ♠Q. He then cashes the ♡A. It is possible that he has the ♡K as well, in which case he will be able to draw all three of your trumps, but there are two possibilities — either East, who opened the bidding, has the ♡K, or South is in a hurry, seeing the impending spade ruff coming. He will be hoping you, West, started with only two trumps. However you play the ♡5 on the ♡A — and East drops the ♡J. When South follows with another trump towards the ♡Q you complete the peter by playing the ♡2. East, as you had hoped, wins with the ♡K, and he doesn't guess or hope that you have a third trump — he knows, because you've said so. So he can safely lead another spade to give you your ruff.

In its negative aspect this signal is almost equally useful. *Failure* to peter in trumps should indicate to partner that either no third trump is held, *or* no ruff is available. This knowledge can save many an otherwise wasted defensive 'tempo'. Had you started life with three spades and three hearts, you would *not* have petered in trumps, to warn partner that it was no use trying to give you a ruff. Similarly, if you'd had two doubletons, one in each major, you would not have petered, and East wouldn't waste defensive time hoping for you to ruff.

Keep this trump peter for the double message 'I have three trumps *and* something I hope to do with the third'. This may even be a ruff in a different suit if partner can be sure you have a trump left.

17 The Acol Strong Two Opening Bid

Playing tricks — Strong Two openings — the negative response — positive responses — opener's rebids — three important questions

You will have gathered by now that, in Acol, we have no truck with the 'phoney club' nonsense, a bid which, for the most part, is made because the player doesn't take time to think of a more descriptive bid. When we bid we mean it, and we try to put partner in the picture as quickly as possible, even if we can't say everything on the first round. This is one of the times when a Strong Two comes in.

Every bid you make should be as descriptive as possible, which in turn means that if you open the bidding at the one-level, you are denying the strength to make a stronger bid so equally, in reverse, if you open at the two-level, you are saying that your hand is better than a one-level opener. Strong Twos are based on playing tricks — eight of them in your own hand. You will also have one predominating suit (possibly two, but we'll take that alternative presently).

Playing Tricks: Don't confuse 'playing tricks' with top tricks or quick tricks which you will meet later. A playing trick is a card which you can confidently expect will win a trick and, in the context of a Strong Two opening, these will mainly be in your long strong trump suit. First, though, learn the important rules shown in the following table:

When considering a Strong Two opening, *don't count points, count playing tricks.*

Strong two openings may be made in spades, hearts or diamonds. They should contain 8 playing tricks in a single-suited hand or, with a two-suiter, the hand should be likely to develop 8 playing tricks if played in the suit which fits partner's hand best.

Strong Two openings are *unconditionally forcing for one round.*

a)	♠ A K Q J 9 7 4	b)	♠ K Q 7	c)	♠ 8
	♡ 9		♡ A K Q J 8 5		♡ A Q J 10 9 6
	◇ A 7 2		◇ 9		◇ A Q J 10 8
	♣ 6 3		♣ A 6 5		♣ A

With hand (a) you can expect to collect seven tricks in spades if they are trumps which, plus the ◇ A, makes eight, so open 2 ♠. With (b) you would be unlucky indeed not to win six heart tricks if you play in that suit, the ♣ A is another, and you will get one, if not two from your ♠ K-Q-7. With (c), surely if your partner can produce a fit for you in either of your red suits, you will win eight tricks. Notice, by the way, that though hand (a) contains eight playing tricks, it has only 14 high-card points, which should underline the reason for not counting points! Hand (c) underlines the reason why an opening Strong Two must be kept open for one round, and that is to give you a certain chance to show your second suit if you have one.

The Negative Response: The negative response, to show something in the region of thirteen peanuts, is 2 NT.

Positive Responses: Holding 1+ honour tricks in a suit that can be shown without raising the level of the bidding (2♡-2♠) is enough for a positive response, but if the response has to be at the 3-level, (2♡-3◇) 1½ tricks plus a biddable suit are required.

There are, however, other vitally important 'positive' responses which you must learn by heart. First, look back at the example hands, and you will realise that opener always has a long strong suit. It may have a gap in it, such as A-Q-J-10-7-6-4, but when counting the playing tricks, opener is entitled to assume a reasonable distribution of the missing cards. Without the king he could count this suit as worth six playing tricks, and would need two more somewhere to make up his eight. But the important thing to remember is that opener won't expect 4-card trump support if you raise him in his suit — two to a high honour will fill the gap, and the most important thing you can tell your partner, if you are able to give a positive response, is that his suit is O.K. by you.

Rules for Responder:

Always give preference to supporting partner's suit if you can.

A double jump by responder (2♠-4♠ or 2◇-4◇) is 'conventional', showing about 10-12 points but *no ace or void.*

A single raise (2♠-3♠ or 2◇-3◇) is constructive and unlimited, showing trump support and *at least one ace or void.*

An immediate response of 3 NT is another conventional bid, showing 10-12 points in an evenly balanced hand, i.e., no biddable suit and insufficient trumps to support partner's bid suit (only x-x – Q-x is enough to support).

The immediate support for partner's suit is invaluable, as is the level at which you bid. For example, if partner opens 2♠ and you bid a direct 4♠, he knows in the shortest possible time that, however good his hand, there is no point in going on to investigate for a slam if he himself is missing two first-round controls, because he will know that you haven't got one. On the other hand, if you raise his 2♠ to 3♠ he will know you have trump support and at least (not *only*) one ace or void, and has plenty of bidding space to investigate if he thinks a slam might be available.

As usual our little set of examples should help to set the scene.

a) ♠ J 9 8 7   b) ♠ K J 8   c) ♠ K 9 8   d) ♠ 7
    ♡ K J 8   ♡ J 9 8 4   ♡ A K Q J 10 6   ♡ 9 7 6 4
    ◇ K Q 7   ◇ J 7 5   ◇ 9 8 5   ◇ 8 6 5 3
    ♣ 8 5 4   ♣ A 9 3   ♣ 7   ♣ 10 7 6 5

On hand (a) if partner opens 2♠, 2♡ or 2◇, raise direct to the 4-level, promising trump support but no first round control. On (b) you have an ace, so mustn't deny it. Raise 2♠, 2♡ or 2◇ to the 3-level and await developments. On (c) it is far better to raise an opening 2♠ to 3♠ than to show the hearts. They will always be useful for discarding opener's rubbish on, and it would even be better to raise 2◇ to 3◇ rather than show the hearts — the least likely second suit for opener to hold. Hand (d) is our highlight on why an opening Strong Two must be kept open for one round. Suppose partner is two-suited in spades and another suit. If you leave him wallowing in 2♠ it may be disastrous, whereas if he has two suits and is given the chance to show the second, you have a 4-card fit for him.

There is one other positive response you must learn, and that is a jump bid in a new suit (2♡-3♠ or 2♠-4♢). As the responses are made in what is known as a forcing situation — the Strong Two opening is forcing — a jump bid in a new suit shows a long, solid, self-supporting suit of your own, as good as seven to the A-K-Q or six headed by the four top honours. This, by implication, denies support for partner's suit (see hand (c) p. 107 where you preferred to raise 2 ♠ to 3 ♠ rather than show the hearts). This jump bid in a new suit occurs in other situations too, and it is far from unknown (we've done it ourselves) to put partner into a slam in his suit when you have a void in it, because you have been told he needs no help from you.

Opener's Rebids: If you open with a *good* Strong Two and are fortunate enough to get a positive response, more often than not you will think in terms of trying for a slam, but alas, in real life partner will more often make the negative response of 2 NT. Opener will rebid, and now it is up to both sides of the partnership to understand what the rebids mean and what the options are. As responder particularly, don't forget that opener made his Strong Two opening not just for the pleasure of hearing himself make the bid, but to alert you to his strength. You in turn will now be able to take a far more optimistic view of even a weak hand — one on which you might even have passed a 1-level bid — and spring into action. Study these six sequences carefully and remember them, so that if you are opener you can judge the best rebid to make, and if you are responder you won't let your partner down when your turn comes round again.

$$2\heartsuit \quad - 2\ \text{NT}$$
$$3\heartsuit$$

A simple 3-level rebid in the original suit is *not* forcing and may be passed. But remember the strength opener has already shown and try to help him into game if you can. Once you've given your 2 NT negative he won't be hoping for great things from you.

$$2\spadesuit \quad - 2\ \text{NT}$$
$$4\spadesuit$$

Obviously responder doesn't have to bid again here. Opener has decided to have a try for game even if you have virtually nothing. He opened 2♠ instead of 1♠, not only to tell you of his strength, but to make sure you didn't pass. He might have got a positive response and gone for a slam but, as it is, he'll settle for trying to make 4♠.

$$2\heartsuit \quad - \quad 2\,NT$$
$$3\diamondsuit$$

Once again this is a non-forcing sequence. Opener is showing a very strong hand with two suits, and all he is asking is that you should tell him the one you like best. With better diamonds you are allowed to pass. With better (or even equal) hearts, put him back to 3♡. It's even possible that, knowing so much about his hand, you will find the courage to put him up to 4◇ or 4♡.

$$2\spadesuit \quad - \quad 2\,NT$$
$$4\heartsuit$$

Your only obligation here, as opener has already bid game, is to see that he plays in the best-fitting suit. You can leave him in 4♡ or put him back to 4♠.

$$2\spadesuit \quad - \quad 2\,NT$$
$$4\diamondsuit$$

4◇ is a jump rebid by opener below game level, and is forcing — you must bid again. You must choose between raising to 5◇ or giving 'preference' to 4♠.

$$2\heartsuit \quad - \quad 2\,NT$$
$$3\spadesuit$$

Opener has rebid in a suit higher-ranking than his first. This is known as a 'reverse' and is unconditionally forcing which means you must choose between raising him to 4♠ or putting him back to 4♡ — whichever you feel will be best. You can be certain that his hearts, which he bid first, are longer than his spades or he would have bid in the natural order, as in the two previous sequences. So even if you've only got two little spades and two little hearts, put him back to hearts.

With this matter of 'preference', that is, putting partner into the one of his two suits that you think fits best with your own hand, *don't* fall into the trap so many learners do. Just suppose that, with this last sequence, your only respectable cards were the ♠K-10 and that your hearts were ♡7-4. You must *not* say to yourself, 'I prefer spades, so I'll put him to 4♠.' Say to yourself, 'Isn't he lucky? I have two good spades which will certainly fill a gap in his second suit, but I also have two hearts which he has told me is his longer suit' — so you put him back to 4♡. Remember length, particularly in the trump suit, is the most important thing of all. If partner has six hearts and only five spades, he'll much prefer to play his game in hearts!

Three Important Questions: As your experience grows you will learn to extend the use of these Strong Two openings to hands which, though they don't quite qualify for our strongest-of-all bids, an opening 2♣ which we are coming to very soon, are just plain too good for a 1-level bid. Don't worry about these bids too much yet — your tutor will guide you through such perils until you are strong enough to stand on your own feet. When you are trying to decide whether to open with a one-bid or a Strong Two ask yourself these three questions:

1) Does my hand contain 8 playing tricks if played in my long suit?
2) Is my hand pretty well certain to develop 8 playing tricks if I can discover which of my two suits partner likes best?
3) Do I really need to force partner to keep the bidding open for me for at least one round?

If the answer to any of these three questions is 'yes', then you have a Strong Two opening.

You will, of course, have noticed that we have never mentioned a Strong Two in clubs. This is quite a different cup of tea and we shall be dealing with it in the next lesson, and very soon after that we shall be giving you the extra hints you need before you go out into the big wide world of bridge and try your hand at a game with strangers. You've lots more to learn yet, of course, but carry on — bridge really is a simple game if you learn the rules simply and never get yourself muddled.

18 Tony's Railway Station

2♣ opening bid — negative responses — No Trump type hands — responses of 3 or 4 of a major suit — 'Stayman' — simple 'Flint' — rebids by responder after 2◇ — opener's rebid of 3 NT — powerful hands based on quick tricks

Come with us now to Tony's railway station. No, we're not mad — that's what the picture at the head of this lesson is. At one side we have a little man standing on the platform waiting for the slow train to London, and on the other we have another little man standing on the 'down' platform waiting for the slow train home. Suddenly down the middle, with a screech and a roar, and all the torn bits of paper and old tickets flying into the air with the rush of its passing, goes a big express train. By the time the two passengers waiting on the platforms have steadied their nerves and brushed away the scraps of paper, their opponents on the express are busily writing down, 'That's 210 for 7♠, 1,500 for the Grand Slam bonus, and 700 for the game and Rubber.' And that, dear boys and girls, is what a 2♣ opening bid is all about.

This is the most powerful bid you can make. It shows a mighty rock-crusher, so powerful that you virtually expect to make game in your own hand and, with just a little help from partner, a slam. It's every bit as conventional as any other conventional bid you've met so far, and possibly even more so, as it has nothing whatsoever to do with your club holding — you might even have a club void. It says, 'Partner, wake up — I've got the goods.'

Negative Responses: You can see almost without being told that if the 2♣ bid is conventional to the extent of possibly containing no clubs at all, it could well be completely disastrous if your partner were allowed to pass. The negative response, which shows less than 8 points, is 2◇, and if you have to make a second negative bid, this is 2 NT. You'll see how and why this works presently. Meanwhile remember that if you are responder and partner opens 2♣, you *must* bid something, even if only 2◇, to give him a chance to get where he wants to go. His rebid will give you a lot more information.

Unless you are a very lucky card holder you won't pick up one of these monster hands very often, but for the occasions when you do it would be a pity if you didn't know how to cope with them. It would mean missing a lot of lovely slam contracts with their big bonuses, so now let's get down to brass tacks about a 2♣ bid.

No Trump Type Hands: When, as opening bidder, you find yourself looking at a veritable picture gallery in an obviously No Trump type hand you may count your honour points. We're going to take two different opening bids here, because the method of dealing with them is exactly the same, the only difference being the precise number of points you hold which will, in turn, let your partner judge what to do.

First we come to a 2 NT opening, which is a No Trump type hand — turn back to your lesson on this if you are in any doubt — containing 20-22 points. Secondly there is a No Trump type hand just a little bit stronger — one containing 23-4 points, and this we open with 2♣ and *rebid* 2 NT to show the extra values. Actually what we have here is a weak 2 NT (if 20 points can ever be called weak!) and a strong 2 NT, but it is important to be able to let partner know which you have.

Both the 2 NT opening and the 2♣ opening followed by a 2 NT rebid, assuming you've had to bid 2◇ facing 2♣, can be passed by responder. By now, however, you will be well and truly aware that you must look at your hand in the light of what partner has told you. If he's said, by opening 2 NT, that he has between 20 and 22 points, then you don't need much to help him make game. With as little as four or five points, you mustn't leave him languishing in 2 NT by passing. For goodness' sake don't sit looking at a couple of queens and a knave and say to yourself, 'How awful — I can't bid on that!' Remember what partner has announced, and that even these little scraps will fill gaps in his powerhouse, and raise to 3 NT.

Similarly, when partner has opened 2♣ and, after your 2◇

negative, has rebid 2 NT, he is telling you that he holds 23-4 points. Even two points from you will bring his minimum total up to 25 points, and you will remember that 25-6 points between two evenly balanced hands will, with any luck, produce a game. So with just one queen you can raise to 3 NT.

This is a most difficult thing for learners to get into their heads, but if you will only remember to relate your hand to partner's instead of just looking miserably at your own weakness, you will see that even one queen facing 23 points may be all the help your partner wants.

There is something new to learn here, and that is that there is no immediate weak take-out available either in direct response to 2 NT or in the sequence 2♣-2◇-2 NT. If you bid a suit, you are giving a positive response which means the auction must go at least to game and possibly to a slam.

Responses of Three or Four of a Major Suit: You may use either of these responses either when partner has opened 2 NT or when he has opened 2♣, you have been forced to respond 2◇, and he has rebid 2 NT. The only difference is that, with the 2♣ opening, he has promised a little more strength so you need a little less.

Facing either sequence, a bid at the 3-level in a major shows a hand which *may* be worth a slam contract if played in your suit, and a bid of four of a major (unlikely when the auction has started with 2♣) is a mild slam invitation on a hand which *must* be played in the suit you have named.

Before we get to examples, there are one or two other rules which must be explained. Firstly . . .

Stayman facing 2 NT or in the sequence 2♣-2◇-2 NT: As your experience grows you may prefer to adopt other ways of seeking for a major suit fit with your partner, but for simplicity's sake at this stage, just remember all you learned about Stayman in Lesson 10, and that you can apply it at this higher level if it seems to you that to discover a major suit fit would make the outcome of the hand safer than if played in No Trumps. You must never forget, though, the rule we emphasised so strongly in that lesson — you must *not* bid a Stayman 3♣ if there is nothing sensible you can do should opener respond 3◇ to deny a 4-card major, or rebid 3♠ or 3♡.

Red suit transfer bids facing 2 NT or in the sequence 2♣-2◇-2 NT:

As we've already said, there is no immediate weak take-out available facing one of these monster No Trump type hands. If you feel you really must make a weak take-out, you do it by using a red suit transfer bid. You're quite used to the word 'convention' now, so know it as a bid which doesn't mean what it sounds as though it means. A red suit transfer is the use of a 3◇ bid as a preliminary to a weak take-out. It has many complications for when you reach an advanced stage of learning, but for the moment keep to the simplest form — 3◇ *demands* a bid of 3♡ from opener. If you really have long hearts in a very weak hand you now pass, and leave your partner to play the hand as declarer in 3♡. If you have a long *spade* suit in a very weak hand, you bid 3♡, asking partner to transfer to 3♠, and now you can pass. Thus you've achieved your weak take-out at the 3-level.

Finally, an all-important rule which must never be broken:

Opener's rebid of 2 NT after an opening 2♣ and 2◇ response is the *only* rebid which is not forcing to game. Any other rebid must be kept open until at least a game is reached.

Before going on to the next stage, let's have a look at some of the promised examples.

a) ♠ Q J 10 7   b) ♠ A Q J 9   c) ♠ A Q 7
   ♡ A J 9   ♡ A J 9   ♡ K J 10
   ◇ K Q 10   ◇ K Q 10   ◇ A Q J 9 5
   ♣ A K 6   ♣ A Q 10   ♣ K 7

Hand (a) adds up to 20 points with the 'plus value' of two tens. It is a perfect 2 NT opener, but add another 2 points somewhere — say the ♡Q instead of the ♡9 — and it would be *too strong* to tell partner you hold a maximum of 22 points, so you would open 2♣ and show your count by your rebid. In the same way, hand (b) is *too strong* for a mere 2 NT opening. Tell partner of your added values by opening 2♣ and rebidding 2 NT. Hand (c) may surprise you a little because it contains a 5-card suit. Your best opening bid is still 2 NT. The hand may end being played in a suit contract, but keep partner in the picture by telling him of your count. Top it up by adding enough points to bring it into the 23-4 point range, and you should open 2♣ with the intention of rebidding 2 NT.

Rebidding by responder after 2♣-2◇-2 NT: As we've already said, you may pass the 2 NT rebid, but it goes without saying that you won't forget how little help opener needs to make his game. We also said that the negative response of 2◇ to 2♣ shows less than 8 points. There is one exception to this, and that is when you have 7 points made up of an ace and a king, even in different suits. The reason is that aces and kings are far more valuable than lower cards, so that your ace and king would be worth a lot more than a 7-point hand made up of two queens and three knaves. So the bidding we show you now will not include an ace and a king in responder's hand. Wait for that until we get to the positive responses.

a) ♠ K 6 3   b) ♠ J 8 7 6 5 4 2   c) ♠ 9
      ♡ J 9 2   ♡ 3   ♡ Q J 10 9 7 5 4 3
      ◇ 8 5 4 3   ◇ 10 8 7   ◇ 7 3
      ♣ Q 7 6   ♣ 8 2   ♣ 8 2

With (a) raise 2 NT to 3 NT without even a pause for thought: 6 points plus a minimum of 20 points must get you there. The same applies if the previous sequence has been 2♣-2◇-2 NT. Just raise to 3 NT, as you haven't enough to aspire to higher things.

With (b), whether partner has opened 2 NT or 2♣, your feeling must surely be that the hand would play more safely in your spades than in No Trumps. Bring the red suit transfers into use and bid 3♡. Partner will make the forced response of 3♠ which you will pass. Now look at (c), the sort really to bring terror to learners' hearts! It is *too good* to bid by way of a transfer sequence which would stop at the three-level. Bid 3◇ facing 2 NT, and then raise partner's forced 3♡ response to 4♡. Had your suit been spades, bid 3♡, and then raise his 3♠ rebid to 4♠.

Now we're going to stop bringing in the 2 NT opening and concentrate solely on 2♣, but before we go on to opener's bid and the positive actions responder can take, there is one other point we must make. As in 'Flint', which you may already know, in the sequence 2 NT-3◇-3♡-3 NT, the 3 NT rebid is the suggestion of a *diamond* slam.

Opener's rebid of 3 NT after a 2♣ opening: This rebid is just a step higher than the rebid of 2 NT which showed 23-4 points. This time opener is showing 25 or more points lacking a long suit. We said that the 2 NT rebid was the only one which could be passed below game level, but 3 NT is already a game contract so, as responder, you can pass if you see fit, but you aren't prevented from taking action if you would prefer the hand to be played in a suit of your own, or think your own values make it worth a slam try.

Powerful hands based on one or possibly two suits: It stands to reason that every time opener picks up a rock-crusher it won't be a No Trump type hand. It may well be based on one or even two good suits, and here you have to learn a different valuation. Although you would find it pretty hard to pick up a hand worth 2♣ without having a high point count, please, *please,* PLEASE don't count points — count 'quick tricks' and playing strength, because a 2♣ opening bid based on suits should fulfil two conditions: it should contain five quick tricks plus playing strength equal to game unassisted. First, though, you must learn the quick trick count:

A-K in the same suit = 2 quick tricks

Ace on its own = 1 quick trick

King on its own = ½ quick trick, so an ace in one suit and a king in
   another = 1½ quick tricks

K-Q in the same suit = 1 quick trick

A-Q in the same suit = 1½ quick tricks.

Other honour cards and combinations count as plus-values, with
   two plus-values = ½ trick.

Tony always said he was a lazy player and found it easier to count losers on a big hand than winners, so he reckoned that if you could count only three losers you had game in your own hand and, if you had five quick tricks as well, you had a 2♣ opener.

a)	♠ A K 7 4	b)	♠ K Q J 10 8 5	c)	♠ A 8
	♡ A 8 7 6		♡ A 7		♡ A K J 10 7
	◇ A K		◇ A 9		◇ A Q 10 9 3
	♣ 7 6 4		♣ A K Q		♣ A

Look at hand (a). You have 5 quick tricks it is true, but if you start counting losers you will find that you have nowhere near the standard for a 2♣ opening. If partner has nothing you could well end up with just your five top tricks, so the best you can possible do is start with a bid of 1♠. Hand (b) is very different. You have only three losers, one each in spades, hearts and diamonds, and you also have five quick tricks, so open 2♣ and make your rebid in spades. Now partner must go on bidding till at least a game is reached. Hand (c) illustrates another type of 2♣ opener, a two-suiter. Open 2♣ for which you have all the qualifications, and whatever partner responds, rebid first your hearts and then your diamonds. There's no need to go jumping the bidding when you've opened 2♣ and rebid in a suit — the bidding must be kept open for you, so take your time about discovering the best final contract, be it merely a game or possibly a slam.

This has already been a long and rather difficult lesson for you. You've learned about the 2 NT opening bid and the bigger bid of the same type on which the opening is 2♣. You've learned about the negative response of 2◇, and the use of Stayman and red suit transfers, not to mention quick tricks and how to value a hand if contemplating a 2♣ opening. There's still a lot to learn, including 'quantitative' raises, positive responses, and the slam conventions you are likely to need with these very big hands. If we told you about them now it would all go in one ear and out of the other, so we'll keep the rest until next week.

Meanwhile, read over this lesson very carefully and make sure that you really understand it, so that we need nothing but the briefest recap before getting on to the new things you need to know.

We've already warned you that there is more to these red suit transfers than we have given you here, but this rudimentary version is enough for you at this stage.

19 Responding to 2♣ Opening Bids

Negative 2◇ — second negative, 2 NT — responder's second-round jump bid — positive responses — quantitative raises — the Gerber convention — the Blackwood convention

---

The requirements for a 'positive' response to a 2♣ opening bid have tended to decrease in recent years. In fact different authorities still have different ideas, so the best we can do is give you some general and obvious rules, tell you to make sure you're on the same wave-length as your partner before you start to play, and assure you that it won't happen very often anyway!

Negative Response of 2◇: The negative response, which denies as much as 8 points, with the one exception if you have 7 points made up of an ace and a king, is 2◇. The reason why we consider an ace and a king worth a positive response is that they are so much more valuable than just any old 7 points made up of queens and knaves. Once you've made your negative 2◇ bid you can always come to life and show any features your hand may have, such as a long suit, but for goodness' sake get in that denial bid first, or it will only be your fault if partner goes cantering away towards a slam in the belief that you have reasonable values.

Second negative of 2 NT: Never forget that what may seem a very poor hand may be a gold mine to opener who has the values for a 2♣ bid, but if you really hold nothing but peanuts and yet are forced to bid again (you *must* keep the bidding open to game if opener rebids anything other than 2 NT), your second negative is 2 NT.

a)   ♠ K 8 4   b)   ♠ J 8 4   c)   ♠ K 10 8 7 6
     ♡ Q 6 3   ♡ 9 7 4   ♡ 9 8 5
     ♢ J 8 6   ♢ 9 8 5   ♢ J 8 6
     ♣ 10 8 7 5   ♣ 10 8 7 5   ♣ 7 2

On hand (a), respond to 2♣ with 2♢, but if partner rebids 2 NT, raise him to 3 NT. Exchange the ♣10 for the ♣Q and now you have 8 points. You have no suit you want to show, but tell opener the good news by bidding 2 NT instead of that wretched 2♢. On (b) you really have no good news to give. If, after 2♣-2♢, opener rebids 2 NT you can pass. If he rebids in a suit you *must* bid again, so have to use the second negative of 2 NT. With (c) you clearly have no better than a 2♢ response to 2♣ but, once having denied the values for a positive response, opener won't be misled if you show your spades. If he rebids 2 NT bid 3♠. If he rebids in any other suit at the two-level, show your spades.

We'll look at one more collection of hands which call for a 2♢ response on the first round, but for something better later.

a)   ♠ 9 7 5 4   b)   ♠ 7   c)   ♠ K Q J 10 9 5
     ♡ 9   ♡ Q 8 6 2   ♡ 8 3
     ♢ 8 7 6 5   ♢ Q 8 5 3   ♢ 8 6 4
     ♣ 10 8 6 4   ♣ K 7 6 3   ♣ 7 2

On (a) after 2♣-2♢, if opener rebids 2♡, use the 2 NT second negative, but if he should rebid 2♠ your hand is far from utterly worthless. He won't be misled if you do the sensible thing which is to raise to 3♠. With (b) you must respond with an initial 2♢, and over any suit rebid other than 2♠, raise to the four-level, showing, as you did in Lesson 17, some strength but no ace or void. If his rebid is 2♠ again, as in Lesson 17, rebid 3 NT — you are much too good for a second negative.

Responder's Second Round Jump Suit Bid: Even if it happens only once in a lifetime, there is one other bid you should learn. Look at hand (c) above. Only 6 points, so you must bid 2♢ in the first place. But what a different hand it is from (c) in the previous example! So here's your rule — a jump bid in a suit following the 2♢ negative shows a long, solid, and self-supporting suit *missing the ace*. Of course if you'd had an ace anywhere in the hand you'd have had a positive response in the first place, so this message is clear.

Positive Responses: These are very simple to learn and if you've got the values for a positive response, that is, an ace and a king or any 8 points, just make the most sensible bid available to you. If your hand contains a biddable suit in addition to the positive requirements, bid it, even if it's only a 4-card suit. After all, you bid 4-card suits at the one-level, so why not at the two-level? If you've got a 'positive' but no biddable suit, then bid 2 NT. There's one thing we feel sure someone will be asking any moment now, and that's what do I do if my suit is diamonds, because 2 ◇ is the negative. Well, all you have to do is bid 3 ◇. You wouldn't dream of doing this on only a 4-card suit — you would have preferred the 2 NT bid, and the same applies if your suit happens to be clubs — you wouldn't respond to 2 ♣ with 3 ♣ unless you held at least a 5-card suit, which is more information for opener. These responses are all so self-evident that we don't need to take up space to give examples. We will, therefore, get on with the next step which is . . .

Quantitative Raises: These are direct raises in No Trumps based on two things, your knowledge of the number of points partner holds when he rebids in No Trumps, and your knowledge — if you didn't know, learn it now — that given reasonable breaks it requires 33-4 points to make a little slam and a minimum of 37 points to make a grand slam. We're back to simple arithmetic again, aren't we?

If partner opens 2 NT he's showing 20-2 points and you would need a minimum of 11 points to take any more positive action than to raise him to 3 NT. Why? Because even opener's maximum of 22 plus your 10 points can't make your combined total up to 33 points. If you have 11 or 12 points, you don't want to be in a slam unless opener is better than his possible minimum of 20 points. In this case you make an invitational 'quantitative' raise to 4 NT which says to him, 'Pass on a minimum — go on to 6 NT with a maximum.' Exactly the same principle applies when the opening bid has been 2 ♣ and the rebid in No Trumps, except that for the 2 ♣ opener, when rebidding 2 NT, the minimum and maximum counts would be 23 and 24. If you have a 2 ◇ negative response you can't possibly be wanting to go to a slam, and even with seven points your grand total couldn't be more than 31, so you'd just raise to 3 NT. However, had opener's rebid been 3 NT, he would be showing 25 or more points. With your possible maximum of 7 points you know you hold a minimum of 32 points, so can well afford to suggest to opener that if he's better than a mere 25 points, you'd like to be in a slam, so once again would bid an invitational quantitative 4 NT.

These quantitative rebids are far more likely to crop up when you have been able to give a positive response, because then you will be in the market with a reasonable number of points. Suppose the auction goes 2♣-2♡-2 NT-? Opener's 2 NT rebid shows just the same 23-4 points as it would have done without your 'positive' except that he is taking his chance to show that he isn't too fond of your hearts but has a strong balanced hand. You may now use the quantitative raise to 4 NT if you think that will be the best denomination to play in, telling him to go on if he has 24 points (obviously because you have 9 points) or stop if he has only 23.

It goes without saying, though we expect it's wiser to point it out, that if you *know* your own hand brings the total to 33-6 points, you should bid 6 NT direct, and not leave it to partner.

Lastly in this section, there's a conventional bid for you to learn, because you might be in the situation of knowing you have a minimum of 36 points between you, good for a 'little slam', but if partner has his maximum rather than his minimum you'd like this to be a grand slam. In this case you make your quantitative bid but at the five-level, 5 NT. This is a demand to opener to go on to 6 NT regardless of being minimum, but to bid 7 NT if maximum.

These quantitative responses, by the way, can be used facing a 1 NT opening, though it is, of course, vital for you to know the exact spread of the opening No Trump bid.

The Gerber Convention: There will, of course, be many occasions when you want to investigate partner's precise ace and king holdings. Here, facing a No Trump opening bid *only,* you may use a response of 4♣ as *asking* for aces. This bid is obviously an announcement of interest in a possible slam and the responses run quite simply in steps:

In such a sequence as 2 NT-4 ♣, opener's rebids to show aces are:

$$
\begin{array}{ll}
4\,\diamondsuit & = \text{no ace} \\
4\,\heartsuit & = 1 \text{ ace} \\
4\,\clubsuit & = 2 \text{ aces} \\
4 \text{ NT} & = 3 \text{ aces} \\
5\,\clubsuit & = \text{four aces}
\end{array}
$$

It is almost inconceivable (between us we've known it once in our long bridge lives) that the 4♣ bidder is going 'slamming' on an aceless hand so that, in practice, a responder's rebid of 5♣ is left free to ask for kings on exactly the same step principle. It is also important to remember that if the 4♣ bidder makes any other rebid than 5♣ when he's heard the answer to his 4♣ question, this is a sign-off bid, and the 4♣ bidder's decision as to the best final contract, and should be left undisturbed by the player who has answered the question.

The Blackwood Convention: There will be innumerable occasions on which either you or your partner wants to investigate for a slam, and to ask about aces and kings, when you're not bidding in No Trumps. This will mean that it is not a moment to use the Gerber 4♣ bid. There are umpteen slam conventions, but the good old 'Blackwood', which everyone knows even if they use one of the more complicated ones, is what you should learn at this stage.

'Blackwood' uses a bid of 4 NT — either member of the partnership may initiate the Blackwood sequence — to ask for aces. The answers to this question are very simple:

In response to a Blackwood inquiry of 4 NT

5♣	= no ace
5♦	= 1 ace
5♥	= 2 aces
5♠	= 3 aces
5♣	= all four aces

It's not a misprint that the response to show all four aces is the same as to show none, as it would not be within the realms of possibility that both partners were 'slamming' without an ace between them! The reason for the bid is that it leaves a subsequent bid of 5 NT to ask for kings on exactly the same scale.

A word of warning about flying off into Blackwood when you are hoping to play your slam in a minor suit. If, for example, you need two aces from partner to make a club slam, and you bid 4 NT, if you get the unhappy response of 5♦ (only one ace) you are driven into 6♣ whether you like it or not. In the same way, if you need three aces when hoping to play in diamonds, a two-ace response of 5♥ drives you to 6♦. You can't wriggle out of this difficulty by converting to 5 NT, because that would be asking for kings!

Although there are a lot more complications you can add as you get more experienced, there are just three more things you must know at this stage. The first is that neither partner should bid a 'Blackwood' 4 NT until the suit in which you are going to play has been agreed, either directly or by inference. Don't worry about the inference bit — your tutor will explain if you can't wait till you get to it in a later lesson. The second is that if you bid 4 NT to ask for aces and follow it with 5 NT to ask for kings, you are giving a guarantee that *you* know all four aces are held between the two hands. After all, you couldn't be bidding 5 NT unless you were hoping to get to 'grand slam', and it would be madness to do this if you knew you were an ace short!

Finally, the third thing you must know, and that is how to cope if you get a disappointing answer to your 4 NT bid and would like to settle for a contract of 5 NT. As we've already said, you can't bid the 5 NT yourself because it would be asking partner for kings, but any bid in a previously unbid suit orders partner to convert to 5 NT. You will realise the significance of preferring to play in No Trumps when you get to playing Duplicate Pairs. Meanwhile let's end this lesson by analysing this auction. Your partner

$$
\begin{array}{ll}
1\heartsuit & - 3\diamondsuit \\
4\diamondsuit & - 4\text{ NT} \\
5\diamondsuit & - 5\spadesuit \\
5\text{ NT} &
\end{array}
$$

opened 1♡ and you made a strong forcing bid of 3◇. Partner agreed the suit by raising to 4◇. Now, with your heart set on trying to reach a slam, you asked for aces by bidding 4 NT but, disappointingly, partner showed only one. Having only one yourself you knew that two were missing. You wanted to play in No Trumps but couldn't bid it because it would be asking for kings, so bid 5♠, an unbid suit, which partner dutifully converted to 5 NT and you now passed.

20 Strong No Trump Opening Bids, and 'Prepared' Bids

Direct raises in No Trumps — weak take-out — 'prepared' minor suit openings — three golden rules

The majority of Adult Education Centres run their bridge courses in three terms of ten lessons each, so this may well be your last lesson of the second term. You have already learned a lot, and we hope, during your holiday, that you will go out and practise some of it with other players than those you have met in your class. There is, however, one weapon you will need in the big wide world, especially if you go to Golf or Tennis Club Bridge Sections, and that is the strong No Trump. We have taught you the weak (12-14 point) No Trump, not only because we think it is a far superior weapon, but because it is far easier to handle. The trouble you are going to run into is the many people who not only insist on playing a strong No Trump, but don't really know how to handle it either. We propose to show you the right way, and we hope you will have the courage of your convictions to stick to it.

We acknowledge freely that it is extremely difficult for a student player to go out into a circle of players who, by sheer weight of years as players, consider themselves expert. They'll tick you off for what they consider mistakes when, in fact, you are perfectly right. They will tell you that you are out of your mind if you insist on leading low from three to an honour of partner's bid suit. 'You must *always* lead the highest of partner's bid suit,' will come the infuriated cry. Arm yourself by rereading and revising Lesson 9. Get if off pat — with reasons — and then if you have the courage say very humbly, 'Well, the Lederers really are rather famous teachers, and *they* say . . .' Enough of this — let's get on with the strong No Trump.

Strict Acol players use 12-14 points not vulnerable and 15-17 points vulnerable, which is known as 'variable'. But many old-fashioned players stick rigidly to 16-18 points throughout. It doesn't really matter — it's just a matter of simple arithmetic. Every one of the rules you learned in Lesson 3 stands without alter-ation, except that you must gear your responses to the fact that the opening No Trump has shown a specific number of points — let's say 16-18 — and that you, therefore, need that many less for your own replies. What would have been a pass facing a 12-14 point No Trump can now be a raise. To give but one example, fac-ing a 12-14 point No Trump, you would pass on 10 points know-ing that your combined count couldn't reach game requirements, but facing a minimum of 16 points, 10 + 16 = 26, and you raise to 3 NT.

Direct Raises in No Trumps:

1 NT weak	Raise to 2 NT on 11-12 pts. but if strong 16-18 pts,
(12-14 pts)	raise to 2 NT on 7-8 pts.
1 NT weak	Raise to 3 NT on 12+ pts, but if strong, 16-18 pts,
	raise to 3 NT on 8+ pts.

Weak Take-Out: Exactly the same applies to the weak take-out of a 1 NT opening. A bid of 2 ◇ , 2 ♡ or 2 ♠ is just as much a weak take-out as it was facing a weak No Trump. The only difference is that what would be a weak take-out facing 12-14 points could well be a jump bid facing 16-18 points.

a) ♠ 10 8 7 6 4 2
   ♡ 9 6
   ◇ Q 8 2
   ♣ 6 3

b) ♠ 8
   ♡ J 10 4
   ◇ J 9 7 6
   ♣ A K 8 6 2

c) ♠ K J 7 5 4 2
   ♡ 10 8 3
   ◇ 8 4
   ♣ A 7

With hand (a) whatever the strength of the No Trump there is no sensible bid other than 2♠, a spot in which the combined hands are far more likely to play with success than in No Trumps. With (b) there is nothing you can do to improve the situation if partner has opened 1 NT weak. You can't bid 2♣ which would get you both wrecked on the rocks of the wrong 'Stayman' bid, so all you can do is pass and hope your values will be in the right places for him. If, however, you hold this hand facing a 16-18 point hand, you can raise direct to 3 NT. Your 5-card suit is bound to be useful and your count must bring your combined hands up into the game zone.

Note hand (c) very carefully. Facing a weak No Trump, even with distributional points added for your long spades, you only have 10 points. You would need partner to have his possible maximum of 14 points as well as everything going well for you, so your wisest course is to make a weak take-out into 2♠. Facing a strong No Trump, however, you must be in a game contract, and this you would prefer to be in spades, so bid 3♠.

You will notice that we have barely mentioned a 15-17 point No Trump. It doesn't matter because all you need to know is the vital number of points you can expect partner to hold if he opens 1 NT. You will remember that you need 25-6 points between two evenly balanced hands to score the nine tricks needed for a game, and will make your passes or raises accordingly.

It goes without saying that you can use the 'Stayman' convention just as we explained it to you in Lesson 10, though also with due regard to the number of points known to be held by your partner.

Before we go on to the big vital difference between handling a weak and a strong No Trump, we should like to emphasise once more that, correctly used, all the bids are precisely the same except that you must remember to make due allowance for the higher honour count held in a strong No Trump. Beware too of the players who have never heard of a weak take-out and consider the last bid in an auction such as 1 NT-2♠ as forcing and forward-going. It isn't — it's a weak take-out. How else can you handle a hand such as (a) above? Rhoda tells a perfectly true story of a bridge party to which we were invited in the early days of our marriage. She cut with a very charming gentleman, alleged to be one of the best players at the Golf Club. A warning bell rang in her mind and she asked what strength of No Trump he liked. 'Sixteen to eighteen points, of *course,*' came the immediate reply. Rhoda said — it was that sort of a party — that if the bidding from her went 1 NT — gasp, it meant she'd forgotten as she was only used to a weak No Trump. She dealt the first hand, picked up a typical 12-14 point No Trump and duly forgot, though she managed to restrain the gasp when she realised what she'd done. Her partner responded 2♠ and Rhoda, thankful to be out from under her crime, passed with alacrity, and her partner, who made all thirteen tricks, looked at her rather as though she'd crawled out from under a stone, which she felt she had, because she'd totally forgotten to ask whether he regarded a 2-level response to 1 NT as forward-going or a weak take-out. And if that doesn't get it into your heads, what will?

Prepared Minor Suit Openings: 'Prepared' minor suit opening bids are an evil which need virtually only be endured if you are playing a strong No Trump. Even so, you will find them very much misused. You will meet people who say they play the 'phoney club' or the 'probing club' or various other such extraordinary concoctions. The plain fact of the matter is that ninety-nine times out of a hundred a bid of 1♣ should mean what it sounds as though it means. This does not, of course, refer to players using 'Precision' or 'Blue' or any other variety of 'strong club' where the 1♣ opening is just as conventional as our 2♣, and must be answered. Playing Acol, or even 'Utility 2♣' which isn't so very different, you must expect your 1♣ opening to be passed if partner can't dredge up even a 1-level response.

You have practically no need for a 'prepared' 1♣ or 1◇ if you are using a weak No Trump, as you will get all the evenly-balanced 12-14 point hands off your chest in one simple limit bid, so easy to handle and so difficult to compete against. If you have more than 14 points, then once again you are in no trouble. You open one of your 4-card suit (you must have one!) and rebid according to your strength as we taught you in Lesson 15. However, if you are using a strong No Trump you've got to find a way of showing a weaker hand and this is most often done by opening 1♣ regardless. It stands to reason that you can't pass on a 13- or 14-point hand, though most strong No Trumpers would pass on a mere 12 points whilst we should be getting in the way as fast as possible with our 1 NT. So they open 1♣ and then make some sort of a rebid when — or if — partner responds, and neither really knows what the other one has.

A 'prepared' club should never be used on less than a 3-card club suit. This is because we use the limit bids with 4-card support and nothing more constructive to say, facing even a minor suit opening, so you don't want to put yourself in the position of bidding 1♣ on a 13-point hand and only a doubleton club, and hearing partner respond 3♣ — where do you go from there? Do you 'shoot' 3 NT, or play in a 2-4 club fit? That's why we allow a 'prepared' 1◇ too, because if you haven't got three clubs *or* three diamonds, you must have a 5-card suit you could bid anyway. Now let's look at some examples:

a) ♠ 9 7 6 5   b) ♠ A Q 7   c) ♠ J 6 5 4
   ♡ A Q 8   ♡ 8 6 5 4   ♡ J 8 7 3
   ◇ K Q 9   ◇ K Q 8   ◇ A K 7
   ♣ K Q 6   ♣ K Q 5   ♣ A K

Hand (a) is a perfectly good strong No Trump opener, but it is too good for a weak No Trump. Open 1♠ — you have no reason to conceal your 4-card suit if you can't open 1 NT — and rebid 2 NT if partner responds 2♣, 2◇, or 2♡. Hand (b) is almost identical except for the 4-card suit being hearts. Open 1 NT if using 'strong' and 1♡ if using 'weak'. Hand (c) is hardly a hand to bid as a major 2-suiter. But to give yourself all possible chances, open 1♡ to make it easy for partner to raise hearts or bid 1♠. If, instead, he bids a minor, you can bid 2 NT. This is really the best way to handle it whether you are using weak *or* strong No Trump. Yes, it's breaking the rule of opening the higher-ranking of equal and adjacent suits, but for a very special reason. This way you won't miss a spade or heart fit, whilst leaving the way open to play in No Trumps if you have neither.

You will see from the above that we are not in favour of opening 'prepared' minors if any sensible alternatives can be found, but you will undoubtedly meet players who will use them, and expect them of you, so here are four hands which you can try to bid if using a strong No Trump, showing alternative rebids according to the response you receive. We hope they will help to guide you.

♠ K J 6   ♠ K 9 7 6   ♠ K 9 8   ♠ A Q 9 7 6
♡ K 9 7 5   ♡ K J 8   ♡ Q 8 7 5   ♡ K 7
◇ A 6 3   ◇ A 6 3   ◇ A 6 3   ◇ 6
♣ A 9 5   ♣ A 9 5   ♣ A 9 5   ♣ A J 10 8 5

1♣ — 1♠   1♣ — 1♠   1♣ — 1♡   1♣ — 1♡
1 NT   3♠   2♡   1♠

or   *or*   *or*   *or*

1♣ — 1♡   1♣ — 1♡   1♣ — 1♠   1♣ — 1♠
3♡   1 NT   1 NT   4♠

Meanwhile bear in mind that your partner should treat either an opening 1♣ or 1♢ as genuine when framing his reply. To summarise, however, here are three golden rules:

---

1)   Never use a prepared minor suit opening if you have a more natural opening bid, which allows for a sensible rebid. This will be influenced by the strength of the No Trump you are using, but you will be able to bid naturally far more often if using a weak No Trump than a strong one.

2)   Never use a prepared opening of 1♣ or 1♢ without at least three cards in the suit, preferably one of them an honour.

3)   Having been forced into using a prepared opening, always make your rebid in No Trumps *unless* responder bids your 4-card suit, in which case you can raise him according to your strength.

---

21 'Avoidance' Plays

The 'safety' and 'danger' hand

We're getting very knowledgeable now, so instead of cringing at the name of today's lesson we'll think about what it means, and how it can increase your chances of success in your contract to a certainty rather than pure guesswork. 'Avoidance' simply means avoiding the slippery road to ruin. When you have got to chance losing a trick, you look for *and recognise* which defender's hand can do you no harm, and which could do you a real mischief, that is, which is the 'safety' hand, and which the 'danger' hand.

To make learning this as simple as possible, let's take only part of a hand. Here we're going to assume that as South, playing in No Trumps, you've got full control of spades and hearts provided the rats don't get at them.

$\diamondsuit$ K 7 3 2
$\clubsuit$ A J 6

```
      N
   W     E
      S
```

$\diamondsuit$ 6 5 4
$\clubsuit$ K 10 8 3

You need tricks from clubs to make your contract, but you're missing the ♣Q. Which way do you take the finesse? At this stage of your learning it may look a pure guess, *but it isn't.* When you finesse, if West gains the lead he could well lead, say, the ♦Q — remember he's seen dummy too now — and if you had the bad luck to find East with ♦A-J-10-x or something like it, you would lose the next four tricks. So you take the finesse from the South hand into East's because if *he* switches to a diamond, he can't do you any harm. Either defender can win with the ♦A, but it will leave your ♦K to win another day.

Now take exactly the same situation, except that we'll move the North and South diamonds: now which is the 'danger' hand?

♦ 6 5 4 3
♣ A J 6

♦ K 7 2
♣ K 10 8 3

East, of course, because if he won with the ♣Q, he could switch to a diamond *through* your king, and you could be unstitched before you had time to do a thing about it.

Obviously these are situations in which your crimes might never find you out, because that dangerous diamond situation might not be dangerous at all. In the first example West might hold the ♦A, leaving your ♦K perfectly safe, and in the second East might hold it, again leaving your ♦K perfectly safe. But just as a simple finesse is a half-and-half chance, so the position of the outstanding diamonds is a half-and-half chance, and why take a chance if you needn't?

This type of play we call by the rather ugly but descriptive name of 'avoidance play'. It is very common indeed, and can always be easily recognized by two trademarks: a *key suit* (usually trumps, or a long suit at No Trumps) in which you may lose a trick; and a *weak suit*, which is open to attack by one, and only one, of the defending hands. The answer is always the same: try to handle the key suit so that, if you do lose a trick in it, you *avoid* losing to the hand which can attack your weakness.

Now let's have a look at some hands from real life and apply the principle we have learned. This should drum it in that a bit of thought at trick 1 is worth a ton of guessing.

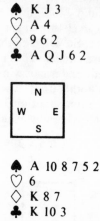

♠ K J 3
♡ A 4
◇ 9 6 2
♣ A Q J 6 2

♠ A 10 8 7 5 2
♡ 6
◇ K 8 7
♣ K 10 3

Here you are South, declarer in 4♠ against which West leads the ♡K. You win it in dummy, as you must, and take stock. You've got plenty of tricks for your contract if nothing disastrous befalls. There are five spade tricks for certain, the ♡A, and five clubs. We've said it before and we'll say it again, the more quickly you grab your tricks without stopping to think, the worse player you prove yourself to be. Remember Lesson 5 where we told you that if you stopped to think at trick 1 the defenders may show signs of impatience, but they'll laugh themselves silly later on when it turns out that you've got yourself into a mess. There's another side to this little picture too. When you're playing against the dragons at the Golf Club and they go down on the hand above, they'll scrabble all the cards quickly together and say, 'Sorry, partner, there was nothing I could do about it — had to lose three diamonds and the ♠ Q as the cards lay.' But there was everything to be done about it and, in fact, 4♠, played correctly, can't be defeated with a hatchet. Go back and look carefully at the hand, discover the danger, and then tell us how you'd overcome it. Right — are you ready?

You've got five certain trump tricks, five certain club tricks, and the ♡A, which is even more than you need for your contract. But you can't make your club tricks till you've got rid of that lurking ♠Q. Perhaps you think the natural way to go about drawing trumps is to cash the ♠A and ♠K, with fingers crossed that each defender has two. If *that* happens you'll make twelve tricks — all very nice, but is it a good exchange for risking not even making ten tricks? Of course it isn't! So we're going to finesse for the ♠Q. But which way? We could play low from the South hand and play North's ♠J when West follows low, or we could cross to dummy with the idea of finessing against East.

What's the 'danger' suit? Diamonds! If East wins a trick with the ♠Q and switches, as well he might, to the ♢Q, you could lose the ♠Q and three diamond tricks. So you cash the ♠K and if, in this particular hand, both defenders follow, you still don't know who has the ♠Q, but if it's West *you don't care.* You can afford to let him win with it because he can't hurt your diamonds. If he cashes the ♢A your ♢K lives to fight another day, and if he leads a low diamond, whether East plays the ♢A or not, you are home and dry, as you're going to make five spades, the ♡A, and five clubs on which you will discard two of your losing diamonds. To rub the point well in, let's look at the full deal as it well might be:

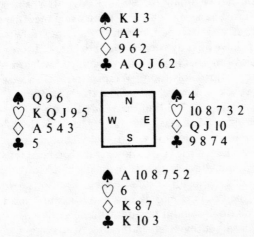

```
              ♠ K J 3
              ♡ A 4
              ♢ 9 6 2
              ♣ A Q J 6 2

  ♠ Q 9 6          N          ♠ 4
  ♡ K Q J 9 5   W     E       ♡ 10 8 7 3 2
  ♢ A 5 4 3        S          ♢ Q J 10
  ♣ 5                         ♣ 9 8 7 4

              ♠ A 10 8 7 5 2
              ♡ 6
              ♢ K 8 7
              ♣ K 10 3
```

The heart lead is obvious. If, as West, you look yearningly at the singleton club, what hope have you of getting East in to give you a ruff? In any case, you hope you've got a spade trick anyway. As things are, East can't gain the lead, but he might, as his only other picture card, have held the ♠Q. In fact, switch a couple of his clubs to West's hand in exchange for the ♠Q-9, and by 'playing for the drop' or carelessly taking the spade finesse into East's hand, you've sealed your own doom.

Here's another one, and this time you, South, are declarer in 3 NT against which West leads the ♡6. East plays the ♡10 and you

♠ A 10 7
♡ 7 5
◇ A K 6
♣ A 10 9 6 2

♠ Q J 8
♡ K J 4
◇ Q 10 5
♣ K J 7 3

win with the ♡J. *Count your tricks.* One heart already under your belt, the ♠A, three top diamonds and four, possibly five clubs as long as you can negotiate the missing ♣Q safely. But what's the horrible staring danger? You know from using the Rule of Eleven that East has at least one more heart, and possibly two, whilst your hearts have already been reduced to ♡K-4. If East gains the lead and plays another heart through you, you will lose all the rest of the hearts — probably four if West started with a 5-card suit, as well as the trick with which he gained the lead. Immediately you give up all thoughts of taking the spade finesse which, if it lost, would give the lead to East, the danger hand, and you decide to concentrate on the clubs. If you're lucky enough to pick up the ♣Q you'll make ten tricks, one more than you need for your contract, but if she wins, and she's in East's hand, do you see that doom looming up again? Yes, of course you do. So you rightly decide to finesse clubs into *West's* hand because he's the safety hand — you don't mind if he does win, he can't harm your ♡K, the only guard you have left in the suit. So having won with the ♡J lead the ♣3 to the ♣A — you never know, you might be lucky and drop the bare ♣Q for no club loss at all — you lead a low club back and unless East pops up with the ♣Q, you finesse the ♣J. You don't mind that the clubs might have broken 2-2, in which case you would have dropped the ♣Q on the second round. The plain fact of the matter is that you can *afford* to lose to the ♣Q as long as it's West who wins, because if he leads another heart your ♡K is good for a trick, and if he leads anything else, you've got your nine tricks buttoned up anyway.

This safety and danger business, even for people who consider themselves good players, is such a grey area, such a source of mistakes which people never even see they've made, that we'll take another example, on the same theme, but of quite a different type. We'll also look at the full deal which, of course, you couldn't do if you were declarer.

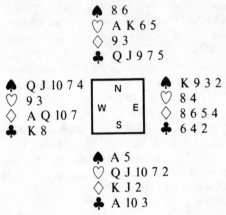

```
                      ♠ 8 6
                      ♡ A K 6 5
                      ◇ 9 3
                      ♣ Q J 9 7 5

   ♠ Q J 10 7 4                      ♠ K 9 3 2
   ♡ 9 3           N                 ♡ 8 4
   ◇ A Q 10 7    W   E               ◇ 8 6 5 4
   ♣ K 8            S                ♣ 6 4 2

                      ♠ A 5
                      ♡ Q J 10 7 2
                      ◇ K J 2
                      ♣ A 10 3
```

You're playing, as South, in 4 ♡ against which West leads the very normal top-of-a-sequence ♠Q. You should never, in bridge, play something just for the sake of playing it, but for a reason, and if you don't stop and think at trick 1 you'll never think of a reason why you must *duck* that opening spade lead. You must stop to think whether there's any danger to your contract before you commit yourself to the possibility of going down. We've given you the hint — the ♠Q will be the top of a sequence, which means that East has the ♠K. In addition, if the diamonds lie cruelly for you as well as the ♣K, you could, as we say, be in the potage.

The answer is to duck the opening lead and now nothing that the defence can do can hurt you. West will probably continue with a second spade — there's nothing better he can do — and now you win and draw trumps. You take the club finesse into West's hand, and he still can't damage your ◇K-J-x. If he's helpful enough to lead a small diamond it will be straight into your tenace, and you'll get rid of your other two diamonds on the established clubs. If he cashes the ◇A he leaves your ◇K good.

Look what happens if you win that first spade. You draw trumps and then have to take the club finesse whether you like it or not. You might be lucky and find the ♣K with East, in which case your crime will never find you out. But if West wins he'll lead a second spade for East to win with the ♠K, and a diamond through your holding will cost you a certain two diamond tricks, which is one trick too many for your contract.

We'll end this lesson with just a little lecture on defence, because when this hand actually came up at the table, South failed to duck, but though he drew trumps ending in dummy at once, he then took, as he had to do at some time, the club finesse. West won and played the ♠J which won because East failed to overtake and switch to a diamond. Thus, though South skidded on this slippery road, the defence also skidded and handed the contract back to declarer. A wide-awake West, particularly if playing with a not very good partner in the East seat, would have led the ♠10. This couldn't cost anything but surely, even if the ♠10 had puzzled East a little bit, he would have got the message that he was expected to win the trick if he could. On lead, he couldn't play a trump, and he could see that neither a club nor a spade was going to do anything for the defence, so for sheer lack of anything else to do, he'd have switched to the fatal diamond.

22   The Range of Responding Bids

Limit bids, single and double raise — direct raise to game — Delayed Game Raise — 'Swiss' responses — 'Blackwood' 4 NT asking for kings — forcing responses

As far back as Lesson 4 we tried to give you an insight into Limit Bid responses in the suit partner opened, that is, a raise in partner's bid suit to show 4-card support and a specific number of points. The values we gave you were 6-9 points for a single raise (1♠-2♠), 10-12 points for a double raise (1♡-3♡) and 13-15 points for a raise direct to the 4-level. All these weeks, if you have been learning with a tutor, you will have had set hands, not only to practise what you have learned in the lesson, but to recap on what you have learned previously. Now having learned to walk, we think you are experienced enough to learn to run a little.

We don't propose to teach you anything new about the single and double raises. They stand on their own merits, and the only addition we expect you to make now is to judge the quality of your responding hand. You can have such a bad ten points that you may judge it wiser to give only a single raise, or you can have such a good twelve points that you judge it better than even a double raise. Now we want to tell you to forget all about a raise direct to game as a strong bid. Although we felt it was all you were capable of understanding without getting muddled in Lesson 4, now you can go on to better things.

Direct Raise to Game of 1♡ or 1♠: In the early days of Acol the immediate raise to game was, as we have taught you, 13-15 points with 4-card trump support. Opener was not expected to take this as a shut-out but, in practice, it was soon discovered that too many slams were missed because opener was afraid to try again. Acol being an eminently sensible system, then, a different use was found for this response, and nowadays it is used purely pre-emptively, that is, as the best possible way to obstruct the opponents. The sort of hand responder should have is one full of 'shape' with exceptionally good trump support.

$$
\begin{array}{l}
\spadesuit \ \text{J 8 7 5 4} \\
\heartsuit \ \text{9 3} \\
\diamondsuit \ \text{K Q 10 9 7} \\
\clubsuit \ \text{6}
\end{array}
$$

This is a typical hand for a raise of 1♠ to 4♠. It is low in point count and high in 'shape', and 4♠ might even be made on a lucky fit with opener. Think, though, of the trouble it may cause your opponents. If your right-hand opponent has passed and your left-hand opponent is itching to come into the auction, he will have to start operations at what may be a dangerously high level. Even if your right-hand opponent has bid — say 2♣ over your partner's 1♠ — it may be extremely difficult for your left-hand opponent to judge what to do for the best over your 4♠ bid. So remember, forget the 13-15 points we taught you when you were babes at the game, and use the direct jump to game as a weak pre-emptive bid.

Delayed Game Raise: It won't surprise you to hear that if you can't show 13-15 points by a direct raise to game, there is another way to do it, and that is via a Delayed Game Raise. You must have your 4-card trump support, and you must have 13-15 points, but amongst your points you *mustn't* have more than one ace. If that sounds odd, don't worry, as we shall explain it when we've got over this Delayed Game Raise. You *delay* your raise to game in order to make it clear to partner that you were too good to put him there sooner. Compare these three examples:

a)	b)	c)
♠ J 9 7 6	♠ J 9 7 6	♠ Q 9 7 6
♡ K 7 3	♡ K 7 3	♡ K 7 3
◇ Q 6 4 2	◇ A Q 6 4 3	◇ A Q J 4 3
♣ 9 6	♣ 9	♣ 9

Hand (a) is clearly within the limits of a raise of 1♠ to 2♠. Hand (b) is better than that. You have 12 points (counting 2 points for the singleton club). You must not, you will remember, bid 2◇, but must show partner the full value of your hand when he opens 1♠, and raise to 3♠. Now look at hand (c). This, facing 1♠, is too good to deny that you hold more than 12 points. So you respond 2◇, merely because that is the convenient suit, and then, whatever partner rebids, you jump to 4♠. Say the auction goes 1♠-2◇-2♡. Partner has not rebid his spades yet, so *he* knows *you* know he may not have more than four. Your next bid must be 4♠, which will tell him everything. You have delayed your raise to game, though you've made it at your second chance, so you must have four spades and between 13 and 15 points.

If the auction has gone 1♠-2◇-2♠-4♠ the message about your 4-card spade support is not quite so clear because this time opener's spades have been rebid, but he will know that you have good spade support for him, and also that even when he has done no more than sign off on the second round, you are not willing for him to play below game level.

The 'Swiss' Convention: You'll remember we said that a delayed game raise response should not contain more than one ace, and that's where the Swiss Convention comes in. Be careful of this, though, because if you go to play with strangers who have played in one little enclosed circle for the last fifty years or so, they won't ever have heard of it, and even if they have, they'll probably tell you it's new-fangled and totally unnecessary. All the same, it's jolly useful, as you will see in a moment. However, another little word of warning comes in here — there are many different variations of the Swiss Convention, so if you do strike a partner who says he knows it, find out if it's the same version as yours as otherwise nothing but disaster is likely to result. As learner players we propose to teach you the simplest version of all, and leave you to read and experiment with others when you feel the urge.

The two responses you will have to learn are 4♣ and 4◇. Both show 4-card trump support and 13-15 points, but 4♣ says that in this basic holding you have two aces, and 4◇ says that you have three aces.

Let's go into this a little further. Using a delayed game raise sequence, *you* knew that you had four of partner's major suit, and you also knew that you didn't propose to let the auction die below game level. Using 'Swiss' you can pass exactly the same message except that you can include in the message the precise number of aces you hold. Compare these three hands:

a) ♠ K 8 6 5 b) ♠ K J 6 5 c) ♠ A 8 6 5
♡ A 9 8 5   ♡ A 9 8   ♡ A 9 8 5
♢ 7   ♢ 7 5   ♢ 7 2
♣ K J 10 9   ♣ A 10 9 7   ♣ A 10 9

With (a), if partner opened 1♠ you would start the ball rolling with 2♣, the prelude to a delayed game raise to 4♠ on the next round. With (b) you have exactly the same point count (13, counting 'shape') but you can pass the message of your two aces by bidding 4♣. With (c), again you have 13 points, and whether partner opens 1♡ or 1♠, can respond 4♢ to tell him of your 4-card trump support and three aces. In other words, you're forcing the issue as far as reaching a game contract is concerned, but giving specific information about your ace-holding.

Your partner, with the information you have given, can simply convert to four of his major suit, or make further forward-going moves towards slam investigations if he thinks fit. You can't learn the whole of Contract Bridge in twenty-odd lessons, so just what moves he could make we'll leave to another term, when you are advanced students. However, there are some obvious things we should like to point out at this point.

Firstly, if you confine your 'Swiss' responses to 13-15 points, opener will know how many of them are tied up in aces. A 4♣ response, for example, showing two aces, ties up 8 points, so it is possible that you could have two kings as well. You couldn't have three kings, because that would bring you up to 17 points, a number which we deal with quite differently and shall be coming to shortly. In the same way, a 4♢ response, showing three aces, ties up 12 points, so it would be impossible for you to hold more than one king in addition to your aces — and if you had one king, you couldn't have a single other picture card at all.

So opener, when you make your Swiss response, already has a lot of information at his disposal, and will probably be in a very good position to judge whether to stop at game or go on to try to investigate for a slam. This brings us to something so common-sensical that students often gasp when they hear it.

'Blackwood 4 NT' to ask for Kings: In Lesson 19 we taught you the 'Blackwood' Convention, which is a bid of 4 NT to ask partner how many aces he holds, and which can continue with a bid of 5 NT to ask for kings on the same scale.

If the auction has gone by way of a Swiss bid of either 4♣ or 4◇, the Swiss bidder has already announced the number of aces he holds. As good sensible Acol players, therefore, it would be folly to ask a question to which you already know the answer. So on any occasion when the specific number of aces held has already been shown, a bid of 4 NT asks for *kings*, not aces which are already known. Thus in the auction 1♡-4♣-4NT-? opener already knows that responder has at least 4-card heart support, 13-15 points, and *two* aces. Why ask for aces again? 4 NT, therefore, asks for kings, and the replies to this question are exactly the same as for 'straight' Blackwood. Similarly 1♠-4◇-4 NT-? is, in effect, asking if responder has even one king, as opener knows he can't have more.

Now turn back to the Rules for Responder on the second page of Lesson 17. Refresh your memories on the fact that a direct raise to the 4-level of a Strong Two opening (2♡-4♡ or 2◇-4◇) shows in the regions of 10-12 *aceless* points. Why ask the question again? 4 NT would ask for kings as it would do in any Acol sequence which has already shown the number of aces, or lack of aces, in a particular hand.

Forcing Responses: Some of you have surely been asking what happens if, as responder, you hold more than the 15 points we've gone up to so far, and that's where a forcing response comes in, a jump response in a new suit. This says quite simply that if partner can open, game is certain, slam is possible.

A word of warning here, one which we have issued a number of times throughout these lessons. *Never bid your hand twice.*

This in itself needs some explanation. To make a forcing take-out (1♡-3♣), other than in exceptional circumstances, you need 16 or more points. Opener, hearing this, should be capable of getting the message, and if you've *only* got 16 points, or perhaps can scrape up 17 points, once you've made your force you've said your little all. Don't *you* be the one to go on pressing towards a slam. Leave it to opener who, if he's worth his salt, has not only heard your force, but translated it, and should surely be the one capable of judging whether to investigate further for a slam or not. That doesn't mean that you must never be the one to press on. If you've got much better than your 16 points, or for some reason really fancy your hand for a slam, by all means bid on. Usually, though, once you've sent your message, all you will have to do is follow partner's lead. If he signs off, then leave it at that. If he asks questions, answer them.

There are certain general rules for forcing, but all of them have to give way to expediency. One thing is certain and never to be forgotten: once one member of the partnership has made a game-forcing bid there is no need to hurry. The auction *must* be kept open to game, and woe betide any one of the two who drops it short of the game target. There'll be only one answer — get a new partner!

The simplest situation on which a force is needed is when responder holds a strong hand and agrees partner's suit.

$$\spadesuit \text{ K 9}$$
$$\heartsuit \text{ Q 9 7 6}$$
$$\diamondsuit \text{ 7}$$
$$\clubsuit \text{ A K Q 10 8 4}$$

If partner opens 1♠ it is wiser to bid a simple 2♣ and await developments — you can always force later if it becomes expedient. But if partner opens 1♡ *you* know the hand must go at least to game in hearts, and possibly to a slam, so bid 3♣. If all partner can do is bid 3♡, then raise to 4♡ and see if he can take it on from there.

Another rule to which you should try to keep, though it isn't always possible, is to force in a suit lower-ranking than the one in which partner has opened. This is to avoid the risk of opener getting enthusiastic about a suit you only used as a means of forcing. If the suit you bid is lower-ranking than his, you can always put him back to his suit until he gets the idea. As usual, some examples should help to clear the air.

a) ♠ Q 8   b) ♠ A K Q J 10   c) ♠ 8
   ♡ A K 10 9 5   ♡ A Q   ♡ A K 10 7 2
   ◇ K Q 8 2   ◇ J 10 8   ◇ K Q 10
   ♣ K 10   ♣ 8 7 4   ♣ K Q 8 4

With (a), if opener bids 1♠, force with 3♡. If opener merely rebids 3♠, raise to 4♠ and see what, if anything, he does next. With (b) if partner opens 1♣ or 1◇, surely a game is certain somewhere? Force with 2♠ — at least tell opener of your strength — and take it from there. He might even like your spades! With hand

(c) be careful. You have a horrible misfit for spades. In spite of your points, bid a quiet 2 ♡ to see what he rebids. After all, it might be a second suit and then you can really go places.

We could go on for hours on these forcing situations but, after all, they are in the higher echelons of bidding which you will reach when you become advanced students. Meanwhile let's end with a few general rules to help you:

Always force when game is certain and slam is possible. Likely situations are:
1) Responding hands with good support for opener's suit plus a strong side-suit which can be used immediately, or established for discards of losers.
2) Single-suited hands with good outside values, where responder feels certain of a safe game contract in his own suit, but can see possible difficulties looming if he doesn't force at once.
3) Hands with 16 or more balanced points which, *ipso facto*, contain at least partial support for opener's suit.
4) Any responding hand on which responder knows where the hand is going, and is certain that it must play in at least a game and possibly a slam.

One final word, referring back to the 'Swiss' Convention. There are many variations of this, so be sure you and your partner are on the same wavelength — otherwise you can land in a heap of trouble.

23 Declarer's Card Management

Recap on making trumps in the 'short' hand — elimination play

As long ago as your fifth lesson we taught you about the simple situations of whether or not to draw trumps. We taught you that you wouldn't gain a trick by ruffing in the 'long' hand, which was nothing but the 'ruff purposeless', but that you could gain many a trick by ruffing in the short hand. Let's just recap on this as a preliminary to taking you a step further on your way to becoming a good bridge player.

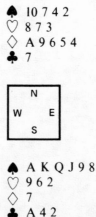

♠ 10 7 4 2
♡ 8 7 3
♢ A 9 6 5 4
♣ 7

♠ A K Q J 9 8
♡ 9 6 2
♢ 7
♣ A 4 2

Here you are South, declarer in 4 ♠ , against which West leads

the three top hearts, and then switches to a trump. You have now
lost all the tricks you can afford and when you see East fail to follow to the first round of trumps, you know that it's going to take
you three rounds to draw them, which would mean only one left
in dummy. *But* you've got two losing clubs — so? You've got to
ruff those clubs in the 'short' hand, dummy, before you draw
trumps. So you win the spade switch in your own hand, cash the
♣A, lead another club and ruff it in dummy. You've still got
another losing club to deal with, but in order to do this you've got
to get back to your own hand. It's clear as daylight that all the
trumps in your own hand are winners, so that using one of them
for a ruff won't turn them into more tricks than they are already,
which is a total of six, but we've never told you that you mustn't
use a trump in your own hand if that is the convenient way of getting back. You've two possible lines of play here, but let's take the
simplest. You've lost one trump in either hand because of West's
switch and you've lost one more in dummy by using it to ruff a
club. With two left, you can afford to serve the double purpose of
drawing one more of West's teeth at the same time as getting back
to your hand. Now ruff your third club with dummy's last trump,
cash the ♢A, and the rest of your trumps are high.

This is pure recapping, but let's take one example to remind
you, and to underline when a ruff in the long hand becomes purposeful rather than purposeless. We're going to change the example hand just a little:

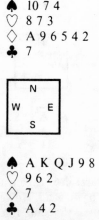

```
        ♠  10 7 4
        ♡  8 7 3
        ♢  A 9 6 5 4 2
        ♣  7

              N
          W       E
              S

        ♠  A K Q J 9 8
        ♡  9 6 2
        ♢  7
        ♣  A 4 2
```

Again you are declarer in 4♠ on the South hand. Just how you got there we're not sure but never mind, once again West leads off with the three top hearts and you've lost all the tricks you can afford. Once again he switches to a trump at trick 4, and once again you've got two losing clubs to cope with. The trump situation is not as rosy as it was before because you're already down to two in dummy; the trumps in your own hand are good for six tricks from now till Christmas, but you need at least one of them to give you an entry to your own hand. Win the trump switch in hand, cash your ♣A and lead another club and ruff it in dummy. Now, *not* to turn your six trumps into seven tricks, but to re-enter your own hand, cash dummy's ◇A and lead a diamond and ruff it. Now you are safely back in the South hand and can lead your last club and ruff it with dummy's last trump.

Now we're really coming to it, aren't we? There *are* useful things you can do with what may be certain trump tricks in the 'long' hand, not a 'ruff purposeless' but a very purposeful one.

Elimination Play: It may sound a bit terrifying, but it isn't really as long as we take it easy. The essence of the manoeuvre is to put the defence into the unfortunate position — for them — of having to help you whether they like it or not. It doesn't only happen at the slam level but slam hands are, perhaps, easier for the learner to see and understand, so here's the first:

    ♠ K 7 4
    ♡ 9 8 7 6 5
    ◇ K 8
    ♣ K 10 6

    ♠ A Q 8
    ♡ A K 4 3
    ◇ A 7 4
    ♣ A J 4

You are South, declarer in 6♡ against which West leads a diamond, which doesn't help you at all. However, if the trumps break 2-2 you'll only have to guess that club finesse right to make thirteen tricks, and in any case will make twelve. So off you go, and cash

the ♡A-K. Alas, East shows out on the second round, so West has
an inevitable winning trump. Now you're on that club guess — or
are you? No, there's something much better you can do about it.
You must eliminate the diamonds so that, when West gets in with
his winning trump, he *must* help you. Lay off trumps, cash your
◇ A, and *ruff your third diamond*. It happens that dummy is the
'long' hand in trumps, but you have achieved your purpose. Next
play three rounds of spades, and it doesn't matter a bit when West
takes his winning trump. You can even afford to put him in with it
now, but because you 'eliminated' diamonds, West can't get off
lead by playing another diamond because he will be giving you a
ruff in one hand and a discard in the other, and the same would
apply if he led another spade. You have deprived him of an 'exit
card' — a card he can play without helping you. His only alternative will be to lead a club, which is just what you want, as it takes
the finesse against the ♣Q for you.

Now here's another one for you, and we really do suggest that
you should have a good think for yourselves as to how you should

```
              ♠ K 10 5
              ♡ A 8 7 5 4
              ◇ 8 2
              ♣ A Q 4


                    N
                W       E
                    S


              ♠ A J 6
              ♡ K Q J 6 2
              ◇ A 7
              ♣ K 6 5
```

play it. Again you are South, declarer in 6♡, and West leads the
◇K which, of course, you recognize as being from at least ◇K-Q.
What's your problem? Hearts and clubs are fine, but you've got
no way of getting rid of that losing diamond, and you've got what
at first glance appears to be a guess as to the position of the ♠Q.
Can you take it from there?

It is, in fact, one of the hands when we wish we could put in a
♠Q in both the West and East hands, so that you couldn't take a

lucky guess and then proudly announce that you'd made the contract. But we can't do that, though we can say that the contract can be made for certain. Got it?

Yes, win the opening lead with the ◇A and draw trumps, which must leave you with trumps in either hand. Now eliminate clubs by cashing three top rounds and then *lead your losing diamond*. Actually it wouldn't matter which defender wins the trick, as either would be in an equally helpless position. He can't 'exit' with a trump, and he can't lead a diamond or club without giving you a ruff-discard, that is, a ruff in one hand and a discard in the other. If he does this you're home and dry, as you can discard a spade, then cash your top spades and ruff the third. So if instead he leads a spade, he takes the finesse for you once again.

♠ K 3
♡ K 10 9 7 2
◇ A K 6
♣ Q 4 2

♠ A 5
♡ A Q J 6 3
◇ 9 8 7
♣ J 5 3

This time as South you are declarer in 4♡ against which West leads the ◇2. Could this be a singleton? Well, we're not going to risk it because we can afford one diamond loser as long as we don't lose three clubs, which could well happen if we have to tackle the suit ourselves. Do you see why? Because unless Lady Luck is very much on your side, if you lead a club towards the ♣Q East could well clobber it with the ♣A or ♣K, and the same could happen to the ♣J. All this needs is for each defender to hold one of the missing club honours and you'll be stuck with three losing clubs as well as a diamond. How to go about it, then?

South wins the first trick with dummy's ◇A and draws trumps, which we'll say takes three rounds as they break 3-0. Never mind — it still leaves us trumps in dummy. Eliminate spades by cashing your two top winners and then go back to the diamonds. Cash your second winner in the suit, then lead your small diamond, dropping your remaining diamond from the South hand. It doesn't matter which opponent wins, as neither defender can get off play with either a spade or diamond without allowing you to discard a club in one hand and ruff in the other, which would mean only two club losers and keep your total losers to three.

The last alternative is for the defence to switch to a club and now, as long as you play *low*, you can't lose more than two clubs.

When you come to p. 175 and learn the 'loser-on-loser' technique you will notice that it is very like the above, but eliminations and loser-on-loser go very much hand in hand.

'Elimination' is such an important part of good declarer play that we'll take one more example to round off this lesson. Let's face it, you can be lucky and take every finesse in sight, and they'll all be right. Thus a bad declarer could make as many tricks as a good one. Frequently, though, the finesses *won't* all be right, and that's where the good declarer comes into his own.

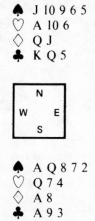

♠ J 10 9 6 5
♡ A 10 6
♢ Q J
♣ K Q 5

♠ A Q 8 7 2
♡ Q 7 4
♢ A 8
♣ A 9 3

You are South, declarer in 4 ♠ and West leads a smallish club. It doesn't look like a singleton but in any case it doesn't help you as you have the three top clubs anyway. You are worried about the ♠K, the ♢K, and a possible two losers in hearts.

It isn't worth messing about with the trump finesse — the ♠K could lie with West, or it could be a singleton, so to start with you win the opening lead and play the ♠A. When the ♠K doesn't fall you play a second spade. Let's suppose that East wins and returns a diamond. Do you take the diamond finesse which, if it's wrong, leaves West with a comfortable exit with another club? No! You go up with the ◇A, because you feel pretty sure that East wouldn't lead low from the ◇K at this stage when he really must have a safe exit with another club. Now you eliminate the clubs by playing off your other two winners in the suit, and then *you* exit by playing your losing diamond towards the ◇Q. It couldn't matter less which defender wins this trick, though it will probably be West, because he'll either have to lead a club or diamond giving you a ruff-discard, or he'll have to open up the hearts, which will mean you can't lose more than one trick in the suit.

If you doubt this last statement, look only at the hearts. If West leads a low heart you play low from dummy. Either East has the ♡K, in which case he'll win with it, leaving your ♡Q and ♡A good for the last two heart tricks, and if East hasn't got the ♡K, your ♡Q will win, as will your ♡A. If, on the other hand, East should be the one holding the ♡K, when he wins with it he can lead a heart if he refuses to give you a ruff-discard. What heart? It doesn't matter, because you play low and if West produced the ♡J your ♡A in dummy will win and the ♡10 will drive out the ♡K, leaving your ♡Q good. If West produces the ♡K your ♡A will take it, and you will be left with the winning ♡Q.

Q.E.D., which every single one of you will remember from your school days, stands for *Quod Erat Demonstrandum* — which was to be proved.

This was a tough lesson. Go back over it, re-read it, and make sure you understand before we take you on to other equally important ways of making sure of your contract.

24 Responder's Rebids

Preference — jump preference — rebids of responder's suit — stronger responding hands

---

If you've done as we have asked you to do, that is read and re-read each lesson until you've got it thoroughly into your heads, you shouldn't find this lesson very difficult. You've heard opener's bid, you've made your response, and now you've got a lot of further information from your partner's rebid. Now it's up to you to bid again.

Of course, your second bid may very well be to pass. Let's take first the very simplest matter of showing 'preference'.

Preference: As usual, some examples will illustrate things best.

With hand (a) you have a weak hand — little more, in fact, than you need to make a response at all. If partner opens 1 ◇ you bid 1 ♠, and if he rebids 2 ◇ you've said your little all and can now pass with a clear conscience. Suppose, however, that he has opened 1 ♡ and after your 1 ♠ has rebid 2 ◇. Are your obligations now over? No, indeed they're not! Do you remember as far back as Lesson 4 the rules for opener's choice of bid? The first of these was, with two suits, to bid the longer suit before the shorter. If, therefore, one of opener's suits is longer than the other, it is up to you to put him back to it. You might not find this difficult if we'd given you three hearts and two diamonds, but with three of each . . . remember he may have more hearts than diamonds, so it's up to you to give him preference to the suit you think he might possibly prefer. Also it's important to remember that this is not giving partner a *raise* in hearts — it isn't. It's no more than a preference bid.

Now let's change the hand slightly. Again, with (b), the auction starts off with 1 ♡ -1 ♠ -2 ◇ . Now how do you give preference? Quite simply by passing 2 ◇ , the suit you prefer. Change the hand once again and this time your original response to 1 ♡ would have been the limit bid of 1 NT. It makes no difference to your obligations. You have heard partner bid two suits, and you must put him back to the one you think he may prefer. He could, of course, have five hearts and only four diamonds, or he could have five of each. Either way make sure he plays in the one he *may* prefer.

Jump Preference: It stands to reason (and by now we hope you have learned what a very reasonable system Acol is) that you can have a responding hand which is better than the ones we've been talking about.

a) ♠ A Q J 7   b) ♠ A Q 9 7 4
   ♡ 10 9   ♡ K Q 7
   ◇ K 8 7 4   ◇ 10 9
   ♣ J 10 9   ♣ 8 5 4

With hand (a) you obviously respond to 1 ♡ with 1 ♠, but when partner rebids 2 ◇ you must raise him. A mere preference you would give by passing, but here it is very easy to see that you must give him a chance by bidding 3 ◇ .

Hand (b) is not quite so easy but your rebid is still perfectly logical. You must give prefererence to hearts but if you just bid 2 ♡, as you did on hands (a) and (c) on the previous example, you will be showing a weak hand with a mere preference — or perhaps not even a personal preference, just honouring your obligation to put partner back to his first bid suit — which is not at all true. You must give a *raise* in hearts by bidding 3 ♡. The idea of this often strikes terror into the hearts of learners, but there's no need for this. It's not a monstrous jump bid showing immense strength, but a simple raise. Partner won't misunderstand. You can't have four hearts or you would have raised 1 ♡ to 3 ♡ on a 10-12 count rather than bid 1♠. He hasn't rebid his hearts, so he may have only four, so he's going to translate your bid into a 10-12 point hand with a spade suit (perhaps only four) and three hearts. Let him take it from there. He can pass, go on to 4 ♡, or perhaps even go into 3 NT. At least you will have told the truth, the whole truth, and nothing but the truth about your hand.

Rebid of Responder's Suit: Now let's take a few examples where your only real values lie in a suit of your own, and see how a slight difference can affect your handling of them.

a)	♠ Q 10 9 8 6 4	b)	♠ Q J 9 8 6 4	c)	♠ Q J 9 8 6 4
	♡ 9		♡ 9 7 2		♡ 9 3
	◇ 9 7 6		◇ 9		◇ K J 8 4
	♣ K J 8		♣ K J 8		♣ 7

On hand (a) when partner opens 1 ♡ you respond 1♠. When he rebids 2 ♡ you could leave him to wallow, but you have a long suit of your own and no support for him, so take out into 2 ♠. In fact go on taking out into spades until he gets the idea. Suppose, instead, after 1 ♡-1♠ he rebid 2◇. Why be selfish? You have three diamonds, so you might as well show preference on this dismally weak hand by passing. Now go on to hand (b). You would respond to 1 ♡ with 1♠, and give preference to 2 ♡ if partner rebid 2◇. If by any chance he'd rebid 2♣, you might well be tempted to show preference by passing, but don't fall into this trap. Partner's hearts are at least as long as if not longer than his clubs, and your club honours are sure to fill a gap, so give preference to 2 ♡. Now let's go on to (c). Here, once again, you would respond to 1 ♡ with 1 ♠, and if partner rebids 2 ◇ you'd show your very real preference by passing. You haven't got enough to raise diamonds to the 3-level — note that opener only rebid 2◇ and made no other stronger bid, either in opening or rebidding, so a comfortable 2◇ contract should suit you very well. Let's suppose, however, that opener rebid 2♣. Now you've got a choice, a repeat of your spades at the 2-level, or a preference to 2 ♡. Which you do is something of a matter of temperament. Probably your wisest course is a simple preference to 2 ♡, though if you think you're a much better declarer player than your partner, rebid 2♠. You'll have only yourself to blame if he is a bit encouraged by this and tries 2 NT. It's worth noting in passing, by the way, that had your diamonds and hearts been exchanged, you would have raised 1♡ to 2♡ in the first place, without mentioning the spades at all.

Stronger Responding Hands: We're coming now to the type of responding hand with which, very possibly because of opener's rebid, you are worth a second try. As usual, we'll take three examples and talk about them:

a) ♠ A Q J 9 2 b) ♠ K Q 10 9 c) ♠ A J 10 7
   ♡ 10 8   ♡ A J 8   ♡ 9 3
   ◇ K J 6   ◇ K J 9 4   ◇ K 10 9 7 3
   ♣ J 8 7   ♣ 7 5   ♣ Q 9

On hand (a) when partner opens 1♡ your obvious response is 1♠, but you have 12 points, on which you could have responded 2 NT. When partner rebids 2♣, isn't it up to you to do something more? After all, you have practically an opening bid facing an opening bid and, particularly with the lead coming up to your hand, you have the diamonds well stopped. It won't take much luck to make a game in No Trumps, so rebid 2 NT. This shows 10-12 points just as it would have done if you'd bid it initially except that you've given even more information to partner. You've said you have a spade suit, a reasonable diamond stop, and 10-12 points. Now opener can surely judge what to do for the best. With hand (b) you could bid a direct 3 NT in response to 1♣, for which you have enough points, but instead you made what could well have been the far more constructive response of 1♠. After all, this change of suit is forcing, so you know you'll get another chance to speak. But when opener can only rebid 2♣ you go straight to 3 NT, which you could have done in the first place. One of the reasons you didn't, of course, is that so often in Acol an opening 1♣ heralds a black two-suiter, and you could miss a possible spade fit completely if you went leaping around in No Trumps.

With hand (c), again opener bids 1♣ and you bid 1◇, your longest suit, first. Many players consider it a crime to conceal a 4-card spade suit, but we think common sense should not give way to hard-and-fast rules. A bid of 1◇ or 1♠ says little or nothing except that you have a 4-card suit, and a minimum of 6 points. Now we get that 1♠ rebid from opener, so we know he has a black two-suiter. It may be 4-4, 5-5, or the clubs may be longer than the spades, but whichever way it is, the rebid has strengthened your hand. You're not *quite* good enough to go direct to 4♠, but you can make the very highly encouraging rebid of 3♠ from which opener will know that he has struck a 4-card spade fit in your hand. It must be a 4-card fit, mustn't it? With five spades you'd certainly have bid them over 1♣. So you must have five diamonds and four spades and, therefore, not more than four cards between hearts and clubs.

It's worth noting, just as a recap, that had partner opened 1♠ instead of 1♣, you'd have made an immediate limit bid of 3♠.

Let's look at just three more examples to round off this lesson. In the light of what you have learned so far, put on your thinking caps and test whether you can find the last bid in each auction before we tell it to you with, as usual, reasons:

a)	♠ A Q J 9 4	b)	♠ A Q J 9	c)	♠ 10 8
	♡ K J 8		♡ K 10 8 2		♡ A J 10 6
	◇ 10 9		◇ K J 6		◇ Q J 9 8 7
	♣ 10 7 4		♣ 10 4		♣ 6 4
	1♡ -1♠		1♡ -1♠		1◇ -1♡
	2♣ -?		2◇ -?		2♣ -?

With hand (a) it is perfectly clear to you that you prefer opener's first choice, hearts. You haven't enough in the unbid suit, diamonds, to suggest a No Trump contract, but you musn't let partner think you **have a** minimum hand, which you haven't so bid 3 ♡ . Had you **held four** hearts with this count you could have made a direct limit bid of 3 ♡ , so partner won't read you for better than 3-card support in a 10-12 point hand. This is still a limit bid, because you couldn't bid 4 ♡ , but not one showing 4-card support.

With hand (b) — did you spot it? — we have the Delayed Game Raise situation we discussed in Lesson 22. You have 4-card heart support for partner, but are too strong to tell him so by bidding 3♡, which is why you chose 1♠ as your first response. In Acol we lay stress on telling the truth and allowing partner to interpret it, so at your second bid you go straight to 4♡. As practically newly starting learners back in Lesson 6 you would have shown 13-15 points and 4-card heart support by a direct bid of 4♡. Now you've gone beyond that stage, and use a change-of-suit response followed by a jump to 4♡.

Now for the last one, (c). You didn't feel any urge to give an immediate raise in diamonds, did you? Of course not. You made what might well be the far more constructive response of 1♡ first. When partner rebids 2♣ your spade holding hardly constitutes a spade stop for No Trumps, but you must do better than give mere preference to diamonds. Bid 3◇, and hope that opener can take further action. If he can't, nine tricks in diamonds is just about what you will find he makes.

We think we should warn you, before leaving this lesson, that there are other responding situations you will have to learn as you go on, 'responder's reverses' and 'fourth suit forcing', to mention only two. Don't worry about them — by the time you are ready to be taught them you will be able to take them in your stride. After all, you are still only in your first year of learning Contract Bridge. We've been at it for more than sixty years, and we can assure you that you'll never stop learning if you are interested enough to go on.

25 Trump Promotion

As we've said before, in real life declarer doesn't bid a comfortable contract and make it. The defenders are sitting there like spiders in their webs trying to weave pitfalls for him. So though opening leads, whether or not to cover an honour with an honour, and defensive signals are all aspects of defence, let's turn to one this week which may be a real eye-opener for you, trump promotion in defence.

By 'trump promotion' we mean exactly that. Quite a small trump can be given the chance to rise from the ranks and take command of the suit. Look at the following example.

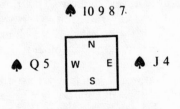

♠ 10 9 8 7

♠ Q 5   N W E S   ♠ J 4

♠ A K 6 3 2

Here, if declarer is allowed to gain the lead, he obviously plays out the top two trumps and escapes with no loser in the suit. Now suppose that, before this can happen, West leads another suit of which both his partner and declarer are void. East trumps in with the ♠J (the essential move in a trump promotion, as we shall see) and suddenly declarer has a trump loser — he can surrender this trick, or he can over-ruff and later lose a trick to West's ♠Q.

Successful trump promotion depends on co-operation from partner, but it's generally pretty easy to spot and even if it isn't, trust partner, who may well really know what he's trying to do! Let's look at a full hand to get the general idea before we turn to particular rules:

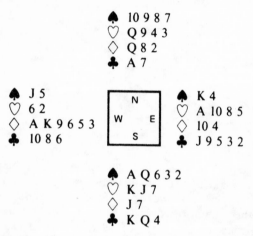

```
                    ♠ 10 9 8 7
                    ♡ Q 9 4 3
                    ◇ Q 8 2
                    ♣ A 7

    ♠ J 5              N              ♠ K 4
    ♡ 6 2                             ♡ A 10 8 5
    ◇ A K 9 6 5 3   W     E           ◇ 10 4
    ♣ 10 8 6           S              ♣ J 9 5 3 2

                    ♠ A Q 6 3 2
                    ♡ K J 7
                    ◇ J 7
                    ♣ K Q 4
```

With South the dealer the bidding has gone 1♠-2♠-4♠ and you, West, lead off with the ◇A-K. What do you do next? You saw East peter with the ◇10 then ◇4, so you know he started with a doubleton and, as you've learned to count up to 13, you know that means South has no more diamonds either. You might lead a third diamond just to prevent dummy's ◇Q from becoming good for a discard, and East can ruff with ♠4. Now, left to himself, South will over-ruff with the ♠6, re-enter dummy and success-fully pick up East's ♠K, and the only other trick he will lose is the ♡A, for 4♠ nicely buttoned up and made.

Now have a look at what *can* happen. East must surely realise that his ♠K is a dead duck and that it might be put to very fruitful use. When you lead the third diamond, *East must ruff with the ♠K*. If South wants the trick he will have to use his ♠A, leaving his only high trump the ♠Q. What's more, when he tries to draw trumps your ♠J won't fall — it will, in fact, have been *promoted* to winning rank. Thus you'll make, as defenders, the two top diamonds, the ♡A and the ♠J.

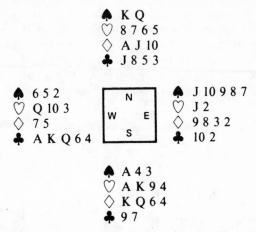

♠ K Q
♡ 8 7 6 5
♢ A J 10
♣ J 8 5 3

♠ 6 5 2
♡ Q 10 3
♢ 7 5
♣ A K Q 6 4

♠ J 10 9 8 7
♡ J 2
♢ 9 8 3 2
♣ 10 2

♠ A 4 3
♡ A K 9 4
♢ K Q 6 4
♣ 9 7

Here's another example with a slightly different twist to it. This time you are defending South's 4♡ and you lead the ♣A. East drops the ♣10 which you read as either a singleton or top of a doubleton so, to test the market, you next play the ♣K on which East completes the club peter. You've got a sure trick in the ♡Q and the two clubs you've already won, but where is a possible fourth trick, to defeat the contract, to come from? If, just *if* you had the luck to find East with the ♡J, it can be used to promote your ♡10 into a second trick. To play the ♣Q would be wasted effort — *you* know that South can over-ruff East, and you also see that all this would do would be set up a master club for South to use for a discard should he want it, not to mention the fact that East wouldn't bother to ruff a winner! *Lead a low club at trick 3.* East must realise that you want him to ruff it, and if he's worth his salt he'll use his otherwise worthless ♡J to do it with. If South wants the trick he'll have to over-ruff with the ♡K and your purpose is accomplished — you have made two trump tricks instead of only one.

One of the golden rules for good defence is never to over-ruff holding a certain trump winner, except on the rare occasions when you need the trick urgently, because even quite lowly trumps can suddenly find themselves 'promoted' if you've refused to part with them prematurely. Because this is not a terribly easy subject, we're going to show you all four hands, but we would ask you to put thumbs over the East and South cards and try to work out for yourself how you should defend, and why, before you study the complete deal.

Having passed as dealer, East came in with 2 ♡, not vulnerable, over South's 1 ♠ and North's 2 ♣. South rebid 3 ♠ and North put him to 4 ♠. Remember not to look at the East and South hands. You, West, lead the ♡8 which East wins with the ♡J and follows with the ♡Q and ♡K, South the ♠10. Do you, as West, over-ruff? Well in this particular instance it won't make any difference.

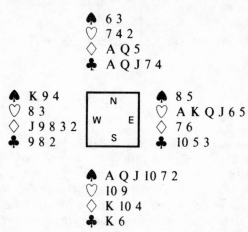

    ♠ 6 3
    ♡ 7 4 2
    ◇ A Q 5
    ♣ A Q J 7 4

♠ K 9 4   ♠ 8 5
♡ 8 3   ♡ A K Q J 6 5
◇ J 9 8 3 2   ◇ 7 6
♣ 9 8 2   ♣ 10 5 3

    ♠ A Q J 10 7 2
    ♡ 10 9
    ◇ K 10 4
    ♣ K 6

Your ♠K is good for a trick, and you can guess that South has the rest of the top spades, so one spade trick is all you're going to get. If either minor suit king is coming your way it will come, and you'll defeat 4 ♠. Otherwise it will make. But now mentally replace East's 8 ♠ with the ♠10, which he well might have. In fact

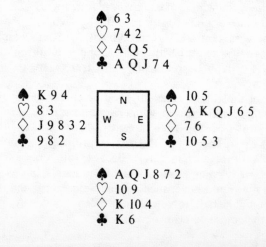

    ♠ 6 3
    ♡ 7 4 2
    ◇ A Q 5
    ♣ A Q J 7 4

♠ K 9 4   ♠ 10 5
♡ 8 3   ♡ A K Q J 6 5
◇ J 9 8 3 2   ◇ 7 6
♣ 9 8 2   ♣ 10 5 3

    ♠ A Q J 8 7 2
    ♡ 10 9
    ◇ K 10 4
    ♣ K 6

having given East the ♠10, look at all four hands, and see the damage you could do to your own cause by over-ruffing with the ♠K if South had ruffed that third heart with the ♠J. Remember his trumps will now be ♠A-Q-J-8-7-2 and he ruffed high because he was afraid you'd over-ruff with the ♠9 and, later, with the ♠K, to defeat him. You'll be playing right into his hands if you over-ruff, because if you refuse what may seem a simple trick, South will be reduced to ♠A-Q-8-7-2 and you will have the ♠K-9-4. South's ♠A will drop only your ♠4, and you will be left with the ♠K-9 over his ♠Q-8 — and all because you refused to over-ruff with what was a sure trump trick anyway. Is it very difficult for you without seeing the hands as they might have been?

There you are. It's not praying for an awful lot if you pray for East to hold the ♠10, is it? And if he hasn't got it, you won't have done yourself any harm by hoping. If he has, you'll have defeated 4♠ when any lesser defender would have let it make. Remember the rule — don't over-ruff with a sure trump trick unless it's really urgent.

♠ A 6 3
♡ 7 4 2
◇ A Q 5
♣ A Q J 7

♠ K 9 4
♡ 8 3
◇ J 9 8 3 2
♣ 9 8 2

```
      N
  W       E
      S
```

This time we won't bother to write in the East and South hands because the situation, and the question, are essentially the same — defending 4 ♠ by South you lead the ♡ 8 to East's bid suit, he wins with the ♡ J and follows with the ♡ Q then the ♡ K which South ruffs with the ♠ J. Do you over-ruff or not?

The answer is no, you don't. Your ♠ K is a trump trick whatever happens later, even though the ♠A is over it. That became certain when South used up his ♠J for the ruff and it also makes it probable that East has the ♠10. So depending on how things go from there, you're certain of one trump trick and could possibly make two, provided you don't fall for the temptation to over-ruff.

A little while ago we said that you never over-ruff with a certain trump trick *unless you urgently want the trick*. It wouldn't be fair to leave it at that without showing you an example, so here we are.

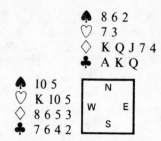

♠ 8 6 2
♡ 7 3
♢ K Q J 7 4
♣ A K Q

♠ 10 5
♡ K 10 5
♢ 8 6 5 3
♣ 7 6 4 2

This time South has only reached a contract of 2♡, but its just as important to try to defeat that as any other contract. Perhaps it gives him game and rubber anyway.

East opened the bidding with 1♠ so you, West, lead the ♠10. He wins with the ♠Q, cashes the ♢A, and then plays off the ♠K and ♠A, declarer, South, ruffing this third spade with the ♡J. The same question — to over-ruff or not? Clearly you have a certain trump trick, but why did East cash that ♢A with all those diamonds staring him in the face on the table? Obviously because his ♢A was a singleton, and it is extremely important to give him a ruff. Nor is this going to cost you that *second* trump trick you've probably already worked out you could get by not over-ruffing. Why? Because East will ruff your diamond return and send back another spade. Your ♡10 beats any trump on the table, so unless South is so desperate for the trick that he ruffs with the ♡Q, your ♡10 will take the trick. If he uses the ♡Q, his only other high heart will be the ♡A and this will not draw your ♡10-5, so you'll get your two trump tricks anyway. In fact South is almost certain to ruff the fourth spade with the ♡Q as his only hope of making the contract, because if you get in again you will lead another diamond, and East is likely to have a second heart to ruff that with too. This would defeat 2♡, so South is going to pray that his ♡Q will win and his ♡A will drop the ♡10 — which it won't!

To round off this lesson let's take one more example, to illustrate another point we've made already — even lowly cards can be promoted to winning rank if the climate is right. It isn't always a case of a 'promotion' staring you in the face, because an error on declarer's part can, amongst other things, be the critical factor.

After an opening of 1♢ from South and a response of 1♡ from North, East had the sense to keep his mouth shut, realising that there was virtually nothing left in the pack for West to hold.

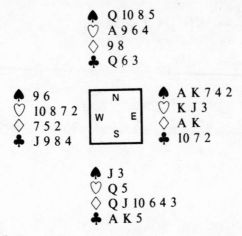

♠ Q 10 8 5
♡ A 9 6 4
◇ 9 8
♣ Q 6 3

♠ 9 6
♡ 10 8 7 2
◇ 7 5 2
♣ J 9 8 4

♠ A K 7 4 2
♡ K J 3
◇ A K
♣ 10 7 2

♠ J 3
♡ Q 5
◇ Q J 10 6 4 3
♣ A K 5

South rebid 2 ◇ which closed the auction, and West led the ♡2. South made the mistake of not counting his tricks, so played low from the table, and East won with the ♡K. East then cashed the ♠A-K, noticing West's peter with the ♠9-6, and led a third spade, on which South had to spare the ◇10. West discarded a small club. Now South started on the trumps, leading the ◇3 to dummy's ◇8 and East's ◇K. East unkindly led a fourth spade, and now South had to ruff with the ◇J. East won the next trick with his ◇A, and if you will check off the cards, you will see that South's remaining trumps were the ◇Q-6 and that West still had the ◇7. The most unkindest cut of all now came from East, who led his fifth spade, and South was helpless. If he ruffed with the ◇Q West's ◇7 was left the master, and if he ruffed with the ◇6, West's ◇7 would be used to over-ruff.

For anyone who doubts about the mistake which allowed this promotion of West's ◇7, we suggest you mark off the cards, assuming that dummy's ♡A went up at trick 1. The immediate lead of dummy's ◇9 followed, when in again, with the ◇8, will result in South being able to afford the high ruffs when East finds the spade switch.

26 Pre-emptive Bids

Opening Pre-emptive bids — Responding to Pre-emptive Bids — Advance Sacrifice — Pre-emptive Opening Four Bids — Countering Pre-emptive Openings

A pre-emptive opening bid is one made at a high level with the sole object of obstructing your opponents' bidding. You don't even hope to make your contract — if you're left there — but you do hope to make life so difficult for your opponents that they miss bidding their own best contract or, in fact, can't bid at all!

Pre-emptive openings, most usually made at the 3-level, are reserved for hands with certain clear characteristics. These are:

a) Practically worthless in defence.
b) Not likely to be valuable to partner as a supporting hand.
c) Likely to be worth 6 or 7 playing tricks at the suit named if vulnerable, and 6 if not vulnerable.

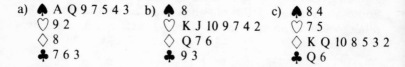

a) ♠ A Q 9 7 5 4 3   b) ♠ 8   c) ♠ 8 4
   ♡ 9 2   ♡ K J 10 9 7 4 2   ♡ 7 5
   ◇ 8   ◇ Q 7 6   ◇ K Q 10 8 5 3 2
   ♣ 7 6 3   ♣ 9 3   ♣ Q 6

The three hands above are all suitable for a 3-level pre-emptive opening. If you open 3♠ on (a), 3♡ on (b) or 3◇ on (c), you can see for yourself that you are not likely to make nine tricks, but you *will* force your opponents, if they want to get into the action, to start at a pretty high level. Moreover you've deprived them of their early rounds of bidding, and they may be quite unable to find their optimum contract.

The best seat at the table for an opening pre-emptive bid is third after two passes. If you hold something like the hands above and both your partner and your right-hand opponent have passed, it's a fair bet that fourth-in-hand will be strong. This doesn't mean that you must never pre-empt as first or second hand, but you would do well to remember that in both cases you will be bidding at a very high level *before* you've heard your partner pass, and it's quite possible that he will be the one in difficulties to know what to do. There are, however, some guide-lines about this situation, which we will come to later in the lesson. Meanwhile, there are some 'dont's' as to suitable hands for pre-emptive openings.

a) ♠ K Q J 9 7 6 3   b) ♠ A Q 9 8 7 6 2   c) ♠ 9 4
    ♡ 8   ♡ J 8 6 5   ♡ 8 3
    ◇ Q 7 4   ◇ 9   ◇ Q 6
    ♣ A 6   ♣ 7   ♣ A J 9 8 6 5 4

What's wrong with (a) for a 3 ♠ opening? Simply that it's much too strong. It's worth practically a 2 ♠ opening (Lesson 17) so you can't even think of telling partner, by opening 3♠, that you hold something like hand (a) on the previous page. You won't know the reason why you mustn't open 3♠ on (b) until you're told — it's that you should avoid a pre-emptive bid on a hand which contains four cards in an unbid major. Here you have a pre-emptive 3♠ opening bid *if* you hadn't got four hearts. Just bide your time and then, if your opponents get busy, bid and rebid your spades until the cows come home. Lastly, what's wrong with opening 3 ♣ on (c)? Well, there's no golden rule about this, and if you feel the urge is too great to resist, or know that your opponents won't know how to cope, by all means open 3♣. It is, however, a fact of life that an opening 3♣ acts rather like a red rag to a bull, and opponents who would hardly dredge up a simple overcall will come into the auction over 3♣ just because they feel you're out to do them — which, of course, you are! Wait till you can open 4♣, or even 5♣!

There's just one other 'don't' which is almost too self-evident to mention. Don't make a pre-emptive opening bid fourth-in-hand. It is pointless to try to obstruct the bidding of three people who have already passed!

Responding to a Pre-emptive Opening Bid: There are bound to be occasions on which your partner opens with a 3-bid before you have had a chance to pass, so all that is really needed is to apply a bit of common sense. You've been told the type of hand your partner has, so clearly you mustn't respond on the sort of values you would need if he'd made a mere 1-level opening. You will, in fact, need something in the region of 3½ to 4 tricks in your hand. With less, you'll just be hoping that your bits and pieces will save him from going too much down. It's also worth pointing out that trump support is the least of your worries. It is just possible that partner has only a 6-card suit, though all our examples are based on 7-card suits, so if you've got big outside values, let him play in his suit — at game-level if you feel you are strong enough to risk it.

Another cardinal rule is never to 'rescue' partner into a suit which may well be less good than his own. Suppose partner opens 3♦, or even 3♠, and you hold a hand like this:

$$♠ \ 5$$
$$♡ \ K \ J \ 10 \ 8 \ 6 \ 4$$
$$♦ \ Q \ 8 \ 5$$
$$♣ \ A \ Q \ 7$$

You haven't anything like the 3½ tricks we've told you are needed to raise an opening 3-bid and nor, even if you exchange one of your other small cards for a seventh heart, have you the slightest assurance that your suit is better than his, or that it will provide a better fit. All you're sorry about here is that you probably hold just too much for it to be possible for your opponents to bid and make a game.

a)	♠ J 6	b)	♠ A K Q J 10 8 6	c)	♠ K J 10
	♡ A 10 9		♡ 7		♡ A Q
	♦ A Q J 8		♦ A K 8		♦ 8
	♣ K J 10 7		♣ 9 3		♣ A K Q J 10 6 5

With hand (a) when partner opens 3♠ (clearly you haven't yet had a chance to bid!) your best bet is to raise to 4♠. You may be a little short of 3½ tricks, but your intermediate cards are all high. Certainly the other side can't bid, let alone make, a game, so you might as well have a bash yourself. With hand (b), if partner opens 3♡, bid 4♠. This can hardly be misunderstood, and you have nine tricks in your own hand, so only need to pick up one from opener to make your game. Now what would you do on hand (c) after 3 ◇ ? The answer is bid 3 NT. You don't want to climb all the way up to a club game, but either a spade or heart lead would give you nine tricks 'on top' and even if opener hasn't got his ◇A, a suit which can be opened at the 3-level is moderately certain to provide a 'stop' so that it can't be run off against you!

Still in the range of responding to an opening 3-bid, there are two simple little rules. Firstly, just as a change-of-suit response at the one-level is forcing, so it is at the three-level. A change-of-suit from a major to a minor (3♡-4♣) is generally used as a slam try in opener's major, and a change-of-suit to a major is game-forcing (3♡-3♠). Neither bid is really capable of being misunderstood by the original pre-emptive bidder. He has shown the character of his hand by his opening so now, if he does have what we call 'a feature', he can show it. We once reached a very comfortable slam by this method. Tony had opened 3♡ − one of his very most inspired efforts on seven hearts to the knave and the ◇A. Rhoda had a rock-crusher including ♡A-K-x-x so bid 4♣ which Tony rightly interpreted as a slam try in hearts. Trusting Rhoda implicitly, he bid 4◇, showing his diamond 'feature'. After all, you can't hold a two-suiter when you open with a 3-bid, and the Lederers were the only pair in the room to bid the 'cold' 7♡.

Advance Sacrifice: Although still in the realms of responding to an opening 3-bid, there's one other point which can bring in many a dividend. In effect an opening pre-emptive bid is an advance sacrifice, because you are prepared to bid something you can't make in an effort to prevent the other side from making something better. In a moment we shall be coming to what you should do if you are on the receiving end of a pre-emptive bid which makes it impossible for you to bid as you would have wished. However, just for the moment let's assume that your partner, South, opened with 3♡ and second hand passed. You hold something like this:

♠ 7 6 4
♡ K J 9 8 6
◇ 10 7 4
♣ 9 3

Do you just sit back and say to yourself, 'Thank goodness he picked hearts'? No, of course you don't — you apply much more positive thinking! You say to yourself, 'My partner's got peanuts except for hearts, hearts and hearts, and that's all I've got.' In other words, the opposition has everything else in the pack, not to mention the fact that if opener has seven hearts, one of them has a void in the suit. What's going to happen? They're going to bid — and make — a slam, so let's make life as difficult for them as possible! Make a further advance sacrifice by bidding 5 ♡, or even 6 ♡ if you have the courage.

This is another hand where the Lederers scored a triumph — Rhoda had opened 3 ♡ and after a take-out request by next hand (we're just coming to that) Tony, on the hand above, bid 6 ♡. The result was that the other pair bid to 6 ♠ which couldn't be made when 7 ◇ was 'cold'. They just hadn't got the bidding space to find out where they ought to be playing.

Pre-Emptive Opening Four Bids: We need just one word about these, because as a defensive weapon they can be very useful. In the minor suits a 4-bid guarantees nothing except a long suit and a desire to make life difficult for the opposition, to go, in fact, a step beyond that red rag situation. A bid of 4 ♡ or 4 ♠, however, is rather different. It shows a hand on which you hope to make game because of your long powerful suit, but it also guarantees *not more than two defensive tricks*. The partner of a player who opens a major suit at the 4-level should take no action on less than two aces. Just one example should suffice:

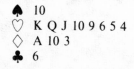

As opener this hand is worth a 2 ♡ opening, as it contains 8 playing tricks, but if partner has already passed, open 4 ♡. This makes it virtually impossible for the opposition to get into the auction, and also warns partner that yours is not a defensive hand. He won't be tempted to make a slam try because, not having enough to open, he can't have enough to put you to any higher contract.

Countering Pre-Emptive Openings: In the previous pages we have seen the damage a pre-emptive opening can do to the other pair, but frequently you will be the ones trying to cope with a pre-emptive opening bid made against you. The methods of doing this are legion, but we propose to teach you only one. It's not the one we necessarily consider the best, but it is the simplest of all, and one which practically every player under the sun will have heard of, and be able to use with you if you cut as partners. Pre-emptive openings were designed to be a nuisance, and a nuisance they will remain. No way of coping with them is perfect, and it is undoubtedly true that, whichever you are using, you will inevitably meet occasions on which you wish you were using one of the others. However, until your experience grows and you are able to read and experiment, we recommend that you should use *3 No Trumps for a take out.* Please turn back to Lesson 12 where you learned that to double an opening bid was asking partner for his best suit — revise this, — and remember that at the high level of coping with a pre-emptive bid, you may well want to double for penalties. We advise, therefore, that you keep the double as a penalty one: 3 ♡ — Double — 'Partner, I don't think they can make it!' Very simple. So when you want partner to tell you his best suit, bid 3 NT over the 3-level opening.

This method, as well as being simple, has the advantage of taking only one bid out of the natural range, and that is 3 NT when you mean it! You can bid a suit naturally over the 3-level bid if that's what you want to do, and you can double for penalties. If you feel you are losing something by not being able to bid 3 NT and mean it, then consider that you could probably double for penalties instead.

Over an opening 3-bid, if you want to hear about partner's best suit, bid 3 NT, and treat it, and your partner's replies, just as you did in Lesson 12 when you doubled to ask for partner's best suit.

Please don't run away with the idea that this is all there is to making pre-emptive openings or countering them. You are still first-year students, and much as you may have learned, there is a long way to go. Take it step by step, and when you become 'intermediate' or even, as we hope, 'advanced' students, you can add the extra knowledge without strain.

27 Card Play Techniques

Most of the material in this lesson you can regard as re-capping, but we know from experience that not only does it take quite a time for various techniques to sink in but, even more important, for you to recognise them when they crop up, so we're going to give you a selection of hands with no more than the essential information about them, and ask you to treat them as quiz problems. Every one has one sensible line of play — can you recognise what this is? *Don't* rush on and read about them without having a real try to sort out the problem for yourself. Let 'think at trick 1' be your passport to success. Here's a very simple one to start with.

Somehow you've got yourself into 6 NT with no opposition bidding to guide you. West leads the ♡Q on which East goes up with the ♡A and instead of continuing with hearts, he switches to a spade. Take it from there and plan how you would play.

O.K. then — off we go. Have you recognised your helicopter? That's the little chap you met in Lesson 7. For a start you dare not take the spade finesse. Apart from the fact that it's highly unlikely that East has led away from the ♠K at this stage, if the finesse loses you are down in your contract before you start. So don't rush away from the table, jump into a taxi and go all the way down to the losing trick factory to buy a loser for yourself when you don't need to. *Count your tricks.* The ♠A, the ♡K, seven diamonds and probably five clubs, although you don't even need

♠ 7 4 3
♡ 7 4
♢ A Q J 10 9 6 5
♣ 3

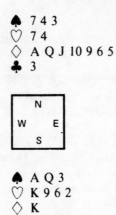

♠ A Q 3
♡ K 9 6 2
♢ K
♣ A K Q J 2

that many! All you need is to recognise your only entry to dummy and it is . . .? Yes, the ♢K. So win the spade return with the ace and, if it makes you feel any better, play off the winners in your own hand. You will, however, get admiring gasps from your partner *and* your opponents if, with perfect calm, you play the ♢K and overtake it with the ♢A in dummy.

You may, perhaps, have noticed that we've given you no clues from the lesson heading as to what you are going to meet in the hands. Can you work out for yourself which technique you need on the next hand?

♠ A K 10 8 6 5 2
♡ 6
♢ 8 4
♣ 7 6 2

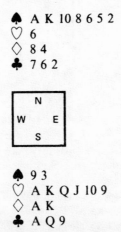

♠ 9 3
♡ A K Q J 10 9
♢ A K
♣ A Q 9

Once again you are South, declarer in 6 NT, and West leads the ♢Q. That's all the information you need. Now what are your problems? You've met this hand, or one very like it, before.

You have eleven top tricks, and at first glance you might think of trying for the twelfth by a club finesse. This, if we filled in the complete deal for you, you would see was nothing but another dash down to that losing trick factory, because when this hand came up in real life West held the ♣K-J-10. There's a much better line to try first and if it doesn't come off, you can always fall back on trying the finesse.

We promised not to bamboozle you with mathematics, but it is practically 90 per cent certain that the four missing spades won't break worse than 3-1. That in turn will mean that one opponent is likely to hold three to a spade honour. Of course, if they should happen to break 2-2 you'd be giving away a trick you could win by cashing the ♠A-K, but what's one trick in exchange for an almost certain way of making the contract? Yes, you win the opening diamond lead, play a spade, and *duck it all round*. Now nothing can hurt you if they break 3-1, and in the horrible event of a 4-0 break, you still have the possibility of the club finesse.

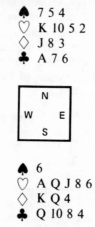

```
              ♠  7 5 4
              ♡  K 10 5 2
              ◇  J 8 3
              ♣  A 7 6

              ┌─────────┐
              │    N    │
              │ W     E │
              │    S    │
              └─────────┘

              ♠  6
              ♡  A Q J 8 6
              ◇  K Q 4
              ♣  Q 10 8 4
```

On this hand East, a notoriously light bidder, opened 1♣, after which by simple stages you, South, became declarer in 4♡ and West led the ♣5.

Now if ever there was a case of buying a losing trick, this was it. How can you go down in 4♡? You've got one spade, the ◇A, and the ♣K to lose. What worse can befall? All this declarer did was to fail to think at trick 1, after which his doom was sealed and he'd made his costly purchase of a loser. Have you done your thinking?

If you have, you will realise that for his opening East must hold the two missing aces and five clubs to the ♣K-J, which marks West's opening club lead as clearly as a singleton as if he'd said it! Refusing any thoughts of 'free' club finesses — you've got plenty of time for those later — you go smartly up with the ♣A and draw trumps ending in dummy. Actually you'll be lucky and find they break 2-2, and *now* you can lead towards your ♣Q-10-x, confident that the worst East can do is duck, so you can return to dummy and do it again.

$$\spadesuit \text{ K 7 5}$$
$$\heartsuit \text{ J 7 6 4}$$
$$\diamondsuit \text{ K 4 3}$$
$$\clubsuit \text{ A K 3}$$

```
    N
 W     E
    S
```

$$\spadesuit \text{ A 4 3}$$
$$\heartsuit \text{ A Q 10 8 3}$$
$$\diamondsuit \text{ A 2}$$
$$\clubsuit \text{ 6 5 2}$$

Here you are again South in 4♡, and West, who bid 3♠ over your opening 1♡, leads the ♠Q. Count your tricks — or your losers if you like — one spade, a possible heart, and a club, so how can you go down in this contract unless you purchase a loser for yourself?

You play a low spade in dummy just in case West started with a 7-card spade suit, and you notice that East drops the ♠8. You've already recognized the ♠Q as the top of a sequence, so all you now have to fear is that East can get in a spade ruff. To prevent this you give up any idea of finessing for the ♡K because if West does get in, and if the ♠8 is a singleton as you suspect, you'll have bought your loser. Now work it out. You can afford to lose one heart trick, but *not* to West, because if West wins and East has a doubleton heart, he will be able to ruff a spade and you'll end up losing a spade ruff, the ♡K, a club and another spade.

This was a hand which came up two or three years ago at the Oxford Congress, and half the room managed to go down in 4♡. In the event the immediate play of the ♡A paid unexpected dividends, because West had the ♡K bare, so South even made an overtrick!

♠ A 7 5 4 2
♡ A K 9 6
♢ Q 10
♣ A 7

♠ 6 3
♡ 8 4
♢ K J 9 8 6
♣ K J 10 4

You are South, declarer in 3 NT and West leads the ♣ 5. A nice free club finesse you think to yourself — or do you? If you do, you've gone down to the losing trick factory in a big way! Where are your nine tricks to come from? One spade, two hearts, a couple of clubs, and surely the rest must come from diamonds?

Have you spotted how your helicopter may crash if you allow yourself what you think may be the luxury of that 'free' club finesse? It will leave you with the bare ♣ A in dummy, and no self-respecting defence is going to let you get away with the diamond tricks. They will hold off the ♢ A until dummy has no more and then any return will leave you locked on the table and down you'll go.

The way to play this hand is to protect yourself from the word go. Win the opening club lead with the ♣A on the table and play the ♢Q. This will be allowed to hold, but you then follow with the ♢10 *and overtake it with the* ♢J in your own hand. Now nothing the opposition can do can hurt you. They can hold up the ♢A as long as they like, or play it as soon as they realize the game's up anyway. You can't be prevented from making a spade, two hearts, four diamonds, and two clubs. Do you see the point? If you win trick 1 with the ♣A, you preserve the ♣7 which you can later lead to your own ♣K as an entry to the diamonds.

The next hand illustrates a technique we have not yet explained to you, so forget about recapping and learn something new.

You are South, declarer in 6♡ against which West leads the

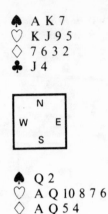

♠ A K 7
♡ K J 9 5
◇ 7 6 3 2
♣ J 4

♠ Q 2
♡ A Q 10 8 7 6
◇ A Q 5 4
♣ A

♣K. We honestly don't expect you to be able to do this one on your own, but at least look at it and try to isolate the problem, even if you can't solve it. Also don't forget to take into account anything you may have learned from the opening lead — because if there had been any opposition bidding we'd have told you.

The problem is your diamond holding, isn't it? Obviously you can get rid of one diamond loser on the third top spade in dummy, but that still leaves you with ◇A-Q-5, and if the finesse is wrong, which it well may be, you'll have two diamond losers. Now let's go back to the clue we tried to give you about the opening lead — West wouldn't lead the ♣K unless he also had the ♣Q, would he?

You win the opening lead in hand, as you must, with the ♣A and draw trumps which isn't going to be very difficult. Even if they break 3-0 you will have three in your own hand and one in dummy left. Now you do two things in one. We've taught you the value of the technique of 'elimination', so eliminate spades by playing first the ♠Q and then dummy's ♠A-K, and get rid of a diamond. Now you're not sitting there contemplating taking the diamond finesse, are you? You were? Well, what about your certain knowledge that West has the ♣Q? Play your ♣J *and discard your ◇5 on it.* West must win, and he can't do anything except lead a diamond into your ◇A-Q, giving you two diamond winners for certain, or lead one or other of the black suits, giving you a ruff-discard, in other words, letting you ruff his black card with dummy's last trump and throw away your ◇Q. Thus you can't lose a diamond trick anyway.

This is called a *loser-on loser* play. The ♣J was a loser and so was your ◊5, whoever held the ◊K. So that's 6♡ bid and made — congratulations!

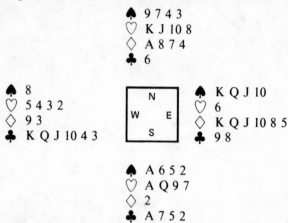

```
                    ♠ 9 7 4 3
                    ♡ K J 10 8
                    ◊ A 8 7 4
                    ♣ 6

    ♠ 8                              ♠ K Q J 10
    ♡ 5 4 3 2         N              ♡ 6
    ◊ 9 3          W     E           ◊ K Q J 10 8 5
    ♣ K Q J 10 4 3    S              ♣ 9 8

                    ♠ A 6 5 2
                    ♡ A Q 9 7
                    ◊ 2
                    ♣ A 7 5 2
```

We don't think it would be fair not to give you the full deal on this hand because not only is it a new technique, but you need to see how very easily you could be on your journey to the losing trick factory. You are South, declarer in 4♡ against which West leads the ♣K, doubtless chosen in the hope that East would be short in the suit. How are you going to make ten tricks in hearts?

If you look at the hand you will see that all your trumps are 'high', and if you can make them separately, that should amount to 8 tricks which, added to your two other aces, make the ten you need. There is, however, a golden rule for what we term playing on a *cross-ruff*, and that is to cash your side-suit winners early. You win the club lead in hand and, to get the cross-ruff going, next play your ◊2 to the ◊A. At this point you could just lead a diamond and ruff in your hand, lead a club and ruff in dummy, and so on. But what will happen? When you come to play the third diamond West will discard his ♠8. Now, when you try to make the ♠A, he will step in smartly with a small trump. Not only are you down to one trump in either hand, but East will have been saving up his top spades, and you'll end up losing three spades and that beastly little trump to West. So remember, when you're going to play on a cross-ruff, cash your side-suit winners before the rats can get at them.

You ought to be able to do this last one on your own so have a jolly good try. Owing to a frightful bidding misunderstanding

♠ A K
♡ —
◇ A K Q 6 5 2
♣ A K Q 5 4

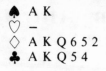

♠ Q J 10 9 8 7 6
♡ A K
◇ 4 3
♣ 3 2

you've ended up as South, declarer in 7 NT when any fool can see that 7♠ would be a cake-walk. West leads the ♡Q. Plan the play.

We'll tell you straight away that East has four diamonds to the ◇J-10-9-8 and that West has four clubs to the ♣J-10-9-8, and neither of them is going to discard from these suits. Every learner's reaction is to discard a small diamond or club from dummy and win the first trick with the ♡K. This is a helicopter hand — you need to build it yourself. Discard the ♠K on the first heart, play the second high heart and discard the ♠A. Now you're there in your own hand to run the rest of the spades and you could make 15 tricks if you wanted them!

28 Bidding After a Take-out Double

The limit bids — conventional 2 NT — a rescue bid — 1 NT — a genuine change-of-suit — redouble

Before you even start on this lesson, go back and thoroughly revise Lesson 12 in which we discussed the 'asking' intervening bids, the hands on which your partner has opened the bidding and your right-hand opponent has made an informatory or take-out double, asking partner to bid rather than telling him in which suit he wants to play. Also you will remember, won't you, that nothing you learn in this lesson applies if the double is of an opening No Trump bid by your partner. The double of a No Trump bid is for penalties and not for take-out. Forgive us for repeating this, but it is all too frequently forgotten.

In addition, of course, to learning what action you should take when your partner's opening bid is doubled, you must also learn to translate the responses if it is *your* opening bid that has been doubled. You mustn't expect your partner's bids to mean the same as they would do without the intervening double.

The Limit Bids: As far back as Lesson 4 we taught you about the values required to make a limit bid in response to opener's bid. In fact you'll find the table on p. 26 and it would be as well to make sure you know it, because now we're going to change it.

It stands to reason that if the player on your right asks his partner a question, you want to make life as difficult as possible for the player on your left, who is expected to answer the question. To do this we *devalue* the limit bids. They must still contain 4-card trump support, but where on 4 or 5 points you would pass partner's opening 1 ♡ or 1 ♠, now after a double, do your best to be obstructive by raising to the 2-level. In the same way, if you would have raised to the 2-level in any case, then after the double, raise to the 3-level. Someone *surely* is going to ask what to do if holding a genuine raise to the 3-level? As usual, we have a very simple answer.

Conventional 2 NT: We'll have a look at some examples in a minute but, in the meantime, if you really and truly would have raised your partner's opening bid to the 3-level if your right-hand opponent had *not* come in with that take-out double, you simply bid a conventional 2 NT. Like all the other bids in this section, this 2 NT is not to be confused with a normal 2 NT response which shows 10-12 points lacking 4-card trump support for opener. It is conventional, showing the full values, including four trumps, for a raise to the 3-level. From opener's point of view it is very easy to deal with. If he would have passed in an auction such as 1♡-3 ♡, he just converts the 2 NT to 3♡. If he would have gone on to 4♡ after 1♡-3♡, he bids 4♡ over the 2 NT. It goes almost without saying that if one player has the values to open, next hand has the values to double, and third hand has a full-strength 3-level raise, there can't be much left for the doubler's partner, so it isn't likely to be necessary to 'pre-empt' him out of the auction.

A Rescue Bid: In an ordinary uninterrupted auction, or one where you are overcalling an intervening suit bid, a change-of-suit is, as you know, a one-round force. After a take-out double it is a rescue bid, telling partner that you have no liking for his suit but that you have a long suit of your own where you think it might be safer to play. A word of warning, though: don't make a rescue bid — that is, a take-out into another suit — if you have reasonable tolerance for partner's suit. Leave well alone — your rescue may well get you deeper into the mire, which isn't difficult to understand if you remember that the double on your right is likely to contain a goodish holding in the suits other than the one doubled.

Now let's have some of these promised examples.

a) ♠ 9 8 6 3
♡ K 7 4 2
♢ J 8
♣ 9 6 5

b) ♠ 9 8 6 3
♡ K Q 4 2
♢ Q 8
♣ K 10 6

c) ♠ 10 7 4
♡ Q J 10 7 6 2
♢ 9 8 4
♣ 7

On hand (a) you would pass opener's 1♡ or 1♠, thankful merely that you have a 4-card fit for him. However, if the hand on your right doubles, make life as hard as you can for your left-hand opponent by raising to 2♡ or 2♠. Opener will know you won't hold your full normal values, so won't be misled. With a few extra points you would raise 1♡ or 1♠ to the 2-level, but after a take-out double you can raise to the 3-level, making it as difficult as possible for the doubler's partner to bid. On (b) you have a full-scale raise of either 1♡ or 1♠ to the 3-level, so use the conventional 2 NT bid. Hand (c) is an example of the possible rescue situation. Without the double you would not even think of bidding, but note the difference according to which suit partner has opened. If it's 1♣ you hate it, and you might as well say so immediately by bidding 1♡. After 1◇ or 1♠ there is no frantic need to rescue. You have three of both suits, so pass and let the future take care of itself.

Now let's get on to the more positive bids, of which there are really three to consider.

1 NT after a take-out double: This bid can be made to show in the region of 6-8 points without any need to 'rescue' or raise the suit opened. It is particularly effective if partner's opening bid, which has been doubled, is a minor, as it obstructs a 1-level reply to the doubler's question.

A Genuine Change-of-Suit response: By this we mean that if, without the double, you would have made a change-of-suit response anyway, now that a simple change-of-suit has become a rescue bid, you must have some means of showing that genuine hand. The point to bear in mind here is that it should be an attacking rather than a defensive hand, which we have another way of dealing with, and shall be coming to shortly. Let's take the above two situations first.

a) ♠ A 5 4   b) ♠ K Q J 9 8 5
   ♡ J 9 8 7   ♡ 7 4
   ◇ 9 7 6   ◇ 9 6 5
   ♣ Q 6 3   ♣ A 5

With hand (a) if partner's opening 1♡ is doubled you would bid 2♡ and, particularly at what we call favourable vulnerability, that is, if your opponents are vulnerable and you aren't, it could well pay dividends to bid a highly pre-emptive 3♡. This really depends on how adventurous you are and whether luck is running your way or not tonight. If partner has opened 1♠, doubled on your right, you create no obstruction by bidding 1 NT, because any bid on your left is going to have to be at the 2-level anyway. But if partner's opening bid is 1♣ or 1◇, 1 NT by you over the double is going to cut out any chance of the doubler's partner bidding either hearts or spades at the 1-level, at the same time as telling your partner that you have better than peanuts.

With hand (b) you would definitely have responded 1♠ over any other suit opening bid. You have an attacking hand — that is, one not really suitable for defence — so, over the double, you bid 2♠, not just 1♠ which would be a rescue bid.

It won't, we hope, have escaped your memory that in an uninterrupted auction a jump bid in a new suit is unconditionally forcing to game (back to Lesson 22 to revise this, please), so that in this new situation the jump bid does *not* carry the same meaning. It is, in fact, a replacement for the simple change-of-suit bid which you can no longer use. It is a one-round force — in other words, partner will treat it just as he would had you responded 1♠ to his suit opening bid. It is *not* forcing to game — only for one round.

Before we get on to the final bid in this lesson, we hope you are noting that each bid you make over the intervening take-out double has its own special meaning. This, of course, is a characteristic of Acol. With a few essential conventional exceptions, we bid what we mean. Rarely is there an alternative, which in turn takes us back to what we have already said: if you make one particular bid it means that you are not strong enough or too strong for another, or that your hand has special features about it which make it suitable for one bid but not for another. Taking this full circle, your partner has to do his share, which means interpretation. So now let's get on to the last bid in this section, and that is the important redouble.

Redouble after a Take-out Double: This bid obviously can't exist at all without the double, so after the double we use it to show a hand unsuitable for any of the bids we have discussed so far. It shows no particular liking for partner's suit, the one which has been doubled, a *minimum* of 9 points, and it also promises to bid once more. It is an invitation to opener to leave this next bid up to the redoubler, because his action may well be to make what will now be a business, or penalty, double, of whatever contract the opposition bids. Opener in turn should take the hint and pass *unless* he thinks his hand totally unsuitable for defence as, for example, if he has a very light opener based on one long suit, or if he has a 2-suiter and thinks that the best prospects for your side lie in a declarer contract of your own rather than in defence.

♠ A J 9 8
♡ 8
♢ K 10 9 8
♣ Q 10 9 7

Let's suppose your partner opened 1♡ which your right-hand opponent doubled. This is the perfect moment to redouble. Your partner will know that you don't much care for his hearts, that you have at least 9 points, and none of the types of hands we've discussed earlier. The redouble does, of course, let your left-hand opponent off the hook of responding to the double, but he may have a suit he thinks it wiser to show. There's nothing to stop your partner from helping to push the boat out by doubling this himself if, with the knowledge you have given him, he thinks it a hopeless contract. He may, however, tell you that he doesn't want to defend by rebidding his hand. He will know he isn't going to get much in the way of heart support from you, but he may have a two-suiter, again with no wish to defend, in which case he will bid his second suit.

The other alternative is that your left-hand opponent will take his chance to pass your redouble, and with anything like a defensive hand *your* partner will pass, from which you will know that he is willing to trust you. It is extremely unlikely that the original doubler will pass and leave the hand to be played in 1♡ doubled and redoubled, in which case he will have to make a bid of some sort. Do you really think he could make 1♠, 2♣ or 2♢ in the face of your partner's opening and what you hold? No, of course you don't, so you honour your promise to bid again by doubling.

Before leaving this lesson it is only fair to say that there are many very competent players who prefer different methods of bidding over an opponent's take-out double. This is fine provided you know what you and your partner are doing and what you mean by your bids — partnership understanding is always vital. You will, however, find that except in very untutored circles, most people will understand the methods we have set out. You would be well advised to make sure you and your partner are on the same wave-length right from the start.

Finally, there are many more situations which can develop, situations where you may not be certain that a double by your partner is intended for a take-out. You can't hope to learn it all at once, so for the time being leave it at the simple positions we have shown you.

Summary

Following a take-out double of partner's suit opening bid:
1) Devalue the limit bid raises — where you would just have passed, raise to the 2-level, where you would have raised to the 2-level, raise to the 3-level to obstruct opposition bidding.
2) With full values for a raise of a 1-bid to the 3-level, bid a *conventional* 2 NT.
3) A simple change-of-suit (1 ◇-Dbl-1 ♡) becomes a non-forcing rescue bid.
4) A response of 1 NT shows 6-8 points and no desire to rescue.
5) A genuine change-of-suit response with a non-defensive hand is shown by a jump in the suit (1 ♡-Dbl-2 ♠) and is a one-round force.
6) Redouble shows 9+ points, no marked support for partner's suit, and promises one further bid, which may be to make a penalty double of the opposition's bid.

---

29 Competing against 1 NT

The pros and cons for a weak No Trump — 'Sharples' — 'Astro' — doubling the opening No Trump — The Anchor Major — responses to Astro 2 ♣ or 2 ♢ — the 'Neutral' suit

As far back as Lesson 3 we extolled the virtues of using a weak (12-14 point) No Trump opening, but that is so long ago that surely it is worth repeating them.

There are three main points in its favour:

1) It is the type and strength of hand you will pick up most frequently and the sooner you get into the action to obstruct the opposition's bidding, the better.
2) It is the most pre-emptive of the opening 1-level bids and, therefore, the most difficult for the opposition to deal with.
3) Strong No Trump addicts will have to be very lucky card-holders to find themselves with 16 or more points more than once or twice in a session. They themselves are unlikely to come to much harm, but they will effectively have warned their opponents against trying to compete.

Admittedly a weak No Trump comes to grief at times, but so can any other contract crash on the rocks of bad distribution, so nothing ventured, nothing won. But having been at pains to persuade you to use a weak No Trump, now we must try to give you some armour against it. Here we're going to stick our necks out and teach you the 'Astro' Convention, for two reasons. The main one is that it's quite easy, quite fun, and the one of the legion of defensive conventions which we personally think the best. The second reason is that almost everywhere you go, at least in moderately untutored or old-fashioned circles, you will find the players claiming to play 'Sharples'. In such circles, however, the convention is so constantly wrongly played and abused that, if we teach it to you properly, you just won't have a clue what your partner is trying to say, or what will be understood by your 'Sharples' bids. We think it's better, therefore, that you should disclaim all knowledge of it, say you've been taught 'Astro' and, if your partner doesn't know what that is, then do without a defensive convention until you have time to discuss it between you.

Doubling the Opening 1 NT: As we've mentioned before, a double of an opening No Trump bid is always intended primarily for penalties. The values required are, of course, dependent on your knowledge of the strength of the No Trump bid, but should always contain two specific things, firstly at least the maximum of the points known to be held by opener, and secondly a promising suit in which to initiate the attack. If you're missing one or other of these, then it's best to use your chosen defensive convention which, as far as we are concerned is Astro, which got its name from the initial letters of its inventors, Allinger-STern-ROsler.

If you feel you can't possibly let opener get away with 1 NT unopposed, and don't feel your hand is suitable for what will be a penalty double, you may bid either 2♣ or 2♢ over the opening.

The Anchor Major: Both 2♣ and 2♢ are conventional, 2♣ showing a minimum of 9 cards between hearts and a lower suit, and 2♢ showing a minimum of 9 cards between spades and any other suit. The major suit thus pin-pointed is known as the 'Anchor Major'. In other words, if you bid either an Astro 2♣ or 2♢ over the opening 1 NT, you promise that your hand is at least 5-4 or 4-5 (possibly more) between the anchor major and another suit of lower ranking value. It also goes without saying that vulnerability must come into it, as you can't stick your neck out if vulnerable, particularly against non-vulnerable opponents — one of the great assets of opening a weak No Trump!

Once you have decided to make an Astro 2♣ or 2♢ bid over the opening bid, it is vital for partner to make the right responses and for you to understand them.

Responses to an Astro 2♣ or 2♢: Whether you have made the

Astro bid, or whether your partner is responding to it, you *both know which the anchor major is,* and as responder you know you can rely on at least four cards in that major suit. You also know that partner didn't consider his hand suitable for a penalty double of 1 NT, almost certainly because he wasn't strong enough for it. With these thoughts in mind, learn these responses carefully:

1) A bid of two of the anchor major promises at least a 3-card fit but shows no game ambitions for your side.

2) A bid of three of the anchor major shows a minimum of 4-card support, is invitational to game but *not forcing.*

3) A bid direct to game (the 4-level) in the anchor major is natural and to play.

4) A pass of the Astro bid (either 2♣ or 2♢) shows weakness with little or nothing besides a long holding (at least six cards) in partner's minor suit bid. Bear in mind that the player who has competed with an Astro 2♣ or 2♢ may have little or nothing in that suit.

5) The 'neutral suit' is the one between the Astro-bid minor and the anchor major. Thus if the bidding has been as in this auction, the anchor major is hearts and the neutral suit diamonds.

S	W	N	E
1NT	2♣	No	?

A bid of two of the neutral suit — 2 ♢ in the auction shown — denies the ability to bid anything more constructive and *also* denies as many as three cards in the anchor major (see No. 1 above).

6) A response of 2 NT to the Astro minor is *forcing* for one round. Generally the Astro bidder should clarify his hand by showing his second suit — remember that the major suit is already known, but not the second suit. 2 NT doesn't promise a further bid, but it suggests that game may be there somewhere. It is, therefore, up to the original Astro bidder to show strength if he has it.

7) A take-out into a new suit, including a jump bid in the neutral suit and a raise in the original Astro-bid minor, is invitational, not forcing, and shows a 6-card suit or better.

8) Using 'Astro', immediate overcalls of 2 ♡ or 2 ♠ can be made naturally. If you really want to overcall in clubs or diamonds naturally, then you must be prepared to rebid the suit at

the 3-level over partner's response to what he supposes is an
Astro bid.

Weird and wonderful can be the tangles either you or your
opponents get into until the bids involved are thoroughly understood. Rhoda tells a true story of days of long ago when she was
playing in a County match between her own County Association,
Berks & Bucks, and Middlesex. Dealer opened 1 NT (weak) and
Rhoda's partner, next hand, bid 2◇. Rhoda duly alerted her
opponents that the bid was conventional, and on request
explained that it meant that her partner held at least nine cards
between spades and another suit. After some thought, with a
strong hand, Rhoda's right-hand opponent decided to pass to see
if she got herself into a tangle which he could double. Far from it!
Rhoda held seven diamonds to the K-Q, passed the Astro 2◇
bid, and there the hand was played — and comfortably made —
when a vulnerable 4♡ couldn't have been defeated with a hatchet
for the Middlesex team. To put it mildly, they were not amused.

It is often possible, because of the cards the player who must
respond to the Astro bid holds, to guess which is partner's
second suit. For instance, on the occasion just related, it was
clear that Rhoda's partner held at least nine cards between
spades, and hearts or clubs, and this sort of knowledge can make
it simpler for responder to judge what best to do. The anchor
major you always know, but sometimes it is impossible to tell
which is partner's second suit. In that case stick strictly to the
rules, so that your partner is not left in the dark. Remember too
that a known number of points are pinpointed in the opening No
Trump bidder's hand, which may make it easier if you or your
partner becomes declarer.

Let's have a look at three likely hands for an Astro bid, and
then three to guide your responses:

	a)	b)	c)
♠	A 10 9	K J 9 8 5	K 9
♡	A J 10 7 4	A 10 9 8	A 10 9 7 6
◇	K 10 8 6	K 8 5	K J 9 6 2
♣	7	6	5

On (a) over a weak No Trump bid 2♣, showing at least 9 cards
between hearts and a minor. On (b) bid 2◇, showing at least 9
cards between spades and another suit. On (c) bid 2♣, showing at
least 9 cards between hearts and a minor. You will notice that
none of these hands qualifies for a double of 1 NT, but all three

are far too 'shapely' for you to want to let opener get away with 1 NT with no attempt to frustrate him.

Now for three responding hands, to make sure you've got the idea.

a) ♠ Q 8 5   b) ♠ Q 8 5   c) ♠ Q J 9 6
   ♡ J 10 9   ♡ J 10   ♡ K Q 8
   ◇ K 8 7 4   ◇ J 10 7 4   ◇ 9
   ♣ 9 6 3   ♣ Q 9 7 3   ♣ A 10 9 7 5

On (a), if partner bids either an Astro 2 ♣ or 2 ◇, simply convert to two of the anchor major. You have no game ambitions, but three hearts *or* spades. On (b), if partner's Astro bid is 2 ◇, convert to 2 ♠, the anchor major. If, however, his Astro bid is 2 ♣, bid 2 ◇, the neutral suit, not because you have four diamonds, but to deny as many as three hearts or any further ambitions. On (c) if partner bids an Astro 2 ◇ you know he has at least four of the anchor major, spades. Bid 3 ♠, highly encouraging but not forcing. If instead his Astro bid were 2 ♣, bid a forcing 2 NT to discover what his second suit is. You already know he has at least four hearts, but if his second suit is clubs you might as well play quietly in a club part-score, whereas if it is diamonds you should have a good play for 3 NT.

30   Duplicate Pairs

*The difference between rubber and Duplicate Pairs —
personal score card — scoring — travelling score slip
— match points — curtain card*

You've now learned a great deal about the basic arts of bidding
and play. We hope you will go on to a second and even third year
of study, but the very best way of improving your standard, and of
learning more, will be to go out into the world of Contract Bridge
and not only to practise what you have learned, but to learn intelligently from other better and more experienced players than yourself. Ask the help of your tutor about this, because anyone qualified
to teach bridge is likely to know what is going on in your area.
There may well be, as Tony and Rhoda had here in our village,
a club which specifically catered for beginners' sessions. There
will almost certainly be a County Association affiliated to the
English Bridge Union, which, if it isn't keen to accept you yet in its
Pairs Championships, may well run special events for the less
experienced. There are many such Associations, and, in fact, Tony
and Rhoda recently presented a special Challenge Trophy, entries
for which are strictly restricted to the inexperienced.

Don't be afraid to try — this is truly your best way of improving
your knowledge as well as your personal performance, and don't
let our next words frighten you off, because what we are suggest-
ing is that you should now graduate to trying your hand at Duplicate Pairs.

We wouldn't want you to go out into the big wide world
completely ignorant of what this means, so in this last lesson we

are going to explain. Firstly, however, note that there are many forms of Duplicate Bridge. Different methods of scoring from what you have learned for Rubber Bridge are involved, but what we want to introduce you to is 'Duplicate Pairs'.

Generally you go to a Duplicate Pairs event with a partner of your choice, but equally generally, Club or County Secretaries will do their best to help you to find a partner. What, though, is the difference? Well, it's very simple. Playing Rubber Bridge you deal the cards for each hand, bid and play, and that's the end of it. Playing Duplicate Pairs each hand, after it has been played at one table, will progress on to the next table, so that each hand will be played over and over again. Don't worry about the actual mechanics of running a Duplicate Pairs — there will be a Tournament Director responsible for all that, so you will start off sitting either in the North-South seats or in the East-West seats, and from that point on you will do just what you are told. You will remain in your seats, or you will move seats, according to the Director's instructions, so you'll have no problems there. What you must learn and understand, however, is the big basic difference between Rubber and Duplicate.

As we've already said, the hand will be played over and over again. If you've been learning your bridge with a reputable qualified English Bridge Union registered teacher, you will already be familiar with duplicate boards or wallets. You will have been playing the prepared hands and putting them back into the boards, or wallets, for the next table to have a go. If you've been learning with someone lacking the basic skills of teaching bridge you won't know what we're talking about, and we're really sorry for you. However, let's make the point that now, playing Duplicate Pairs, although you will probably deal the first set of boards yourselves, you will be taking back your own card at the end of each trick, so that you can return to the board the exact thirteen cards you took out of it in the first place. That will mean that exactly the same hand will go on to the next table.

After each set of boards (probably three or four to a set) you will change opponents. A very ordinary way of organizing this is for the North-South pairs to sit still throughout the session, the East-West pairs to move up one table at the end of each round, and the boards to move down one table.

Do you see what the effect of this is? Unlike Rubber bridge, where you are playing against the other pair at your table, now you will be playing against all the other pairs sitting on your compass points. Your result on any particular board will depend solely on whether you did better on the hand than they did, or worse.

Clearly you'll be in a complete fog at this moment as to what on earth we mean, but to explain it shouldn't be too hard. First, though, let's emphasise a few little points which are all-important in Duplicate. You will be given a 'personal score card' on which you are expected to set out your bidding system in detail. This must be available to your opponents at all times, because it is highly unethical for you and your partner to understand more about your bidding, signals or discards than they do. You are also under an absolute obligation, unless your opponents have told you they don't want you to do so, to alert them if you know your partner has made a conventional bid and to explain its meaning if you are asked to do so.

$$\begin{array}{cccc} S & W & N & E \\ 1\spadesuit & No & 4\clubsuit & ? \end{array}$$

An 'alert' is given by rapping the table so if, perhaps, the bidding has gone like this, and you, South, know that 4♣ is a conventional 'Swiss' bid (revise this from Lesson 22 if you are in any doubt) you, South, must rap the table to alert East that the 4♣ bid was conventional, and allow him the chance to ask you to explain it — if he wants you to — before he gets into a mess. In other words, he must be just as aware of what the 4♣ bid means as you, South, are.

The other important difference with Duplicate of any sort is that the opening lead must be made face downwards. This isn't nearly as stupid as it sounds, because, taking you as the opening leader, if your partner wants to ask questions about the opponents' bidding, he can do so without in any way influencing your lead. He may have no questions, in which case he will say so, you will turn your lead card face up, dummy will go down in the normal way, and play will proceed. If there are questions it won't make any difference to what you lead— you've led it. After any questions from partner you will face your lead and get on with the rest of the hand.

Now before we get on to the actual play, let's look at the difference between the scoring of Duplicate and Rubber. The latter you know all about. The former you've got to learn.

Firstly, there are no rubbers to be won or lost. Each board is a separate entity on its own. The same principle of scoring towards a game only what you bid applies, except that the final score on any one board is all added into one. The penalties for failure in your contract are the same as those for Rubber Bridge but at Duplicate, if you bid a part-score *and make it,* you add 50 points. Thus if you bid and make 2♠ you score 30+ 30 + 50 = 110 points, and for any 'overtricks' that is, for example, bidding 2♠ and making 3♠ or perhaps 4♠, you would only add the trick score of 30 points per trick, so 2♠ bid and 3♠ made would score 30 + 30 + 30 + 50 = 140.

If you bid and make a non-vulnerable game you add 300 points to the trick score, and if you bid and make a vulnerable game you add 500 points. Thus 4♡ bid and made non-vulnerable = 4 x 30 + 300 = 420 points, and 4♠ bid and made with an overtrick if vulnerable would score 4 x 30 = 120 + 30 for the overtrick = 150 + 500 for the vulnerable game = 650 points. Slam bonus points are the same as for Rubber Bridge. Honours do not count.

You will very quickly pick up the way to fill in your personal score card, so now let's plunge right into the final little mystery, the 'travelling score slip'. This is a slip which travels round the room with the board — and which you mustn't on any account look at until you've finished playing the board — and which is the one which gives all the information to the Tournament Director and scorers. Let's start quite simply by assuming that you are playing Board 1 and that, therefore, you have had no movement of opponents or hands. If you are North-South No. 1 you will be playing against East-West No. 1. All the scores are entered from the North-South point of view, either plus or minus. So here we go:

Board No. 1

North Player enters N-S + /- score only

NS Pair No.	E-W Pair No.	Contract	By	North-South		NS Match Points	E-W Match Points
				Plus	Minus		
1	1	4♡	S	420		4	4
2	3	4♡ + 1	S	450		8	0
3	5	4♡ - 1	S		50	0	8
4	2	3NT + 1	N	430		6	2
5	4	5♢ Dbld - 2	E	300		2	6
6							
7							

Let's imagine that we are playing the first board of a 5-table pairs duplicate. Forget about the last two columns on the travelling score slip for the moment as they are for the *exclusive* use of the scorers. Which North-South pair did the best on this hand? Clearly N-S 2 who made an overtrick in 4♡ for a score of +450. Second were Pair No. 4 who made an overtrick in 3 NT so scored 430 points, just a little better than N-S 1 who bid and made 4♡ for +420. E-W No. 4 had a bash at a 'sacrifice' which cost them 300 points, or +300 to N-S 5, and N-S 3 disgraced themselves by going one down in 4 ♡ for -50 — or did the East-West pair find a brilliant line of defence (perhaps a trump promotion such as we learned in Lesson 25) which no one else spotted, to defeat them?

You might think that, playing duplicate, all the luck of being dealt good or bad cards is eliminated. To a great extent it is, but it's impossible entirely to eliminate all luck — how did it happen that N-S No. 2 made one more trick than N-S No. 1? How did it happen that N-S No. 3 didn't make 4♡ at all — was it their bad play or brilliant defence by E-W No. 5? Whatever the answer, a lot of luck has been eliminated which is, perhaps, why Duplicate is becoming more and more popular.

Earlier we said that the final two columns on the travelling score slip were for the exclusive use of the scorers, but you will see that there are figures in them — put there by the scorers. You'll need to understand these before you can play Duplicate Pairs with any pleasure, so here goes. Look at the slip — what's the *worst* score from the North-South point of view? That -50 for N-S. No. 3, so we give them nought, or no Match Points, which is the way we score this type of event. What's the second worst score for North-South? Pair 5 were plus only 300 so we give them 2 Match Points. We score in 2s, by the way, to do away with the complications of ½-points if two pairs get exactly the same score. N-S No. 1 got the next best score, +420, so we give them 4 MP. Next 6 MP for N-S No. 4 for their +430, and top of the list, 8 MP for N-S No. 2 who got the best score of all.

You will see that the 'bottom' score of 0 MP runs upwards to 8 MP, 2 MP less than the total number of pairs playing the board, in this case 5. So the best pair get 8 MP or 'a top'. We can't leave the East-West pairs with no points at all so we do the obvious, give them each the reciprocal points which add the scores up to the possible 'top'. Thus looking at it from the East-West point of view, E-W No. 3 got the worst score and, therefore, the reciprocal of 8 MP which is 0 MP, and so on.

The scorers, under the eagle eye of the Tournament Director, gather all the travelling score slips and extract onto a master chart the total number of Match Points scored by each pair so that, in this type of event, you will find that you have two winners, the North-South pair with the best total of Match Points, and the East-West pair with the best total.

The player sitting North, by the way, is the one responsible for entering up the travelling score slip when the hand has been played, but it is also the responsibility of East and West to see that it has been done correctly. You can see, can't you, that one little error such as scoring N-S No. 2 as making only 4 ♡ instead of 4 ♡ + 1 could make a tremendous difference? It would reduce N-S No.2 to 420 points leaving North-South 4, with their +430 points, with the 'top' of 8 MP. N-S 1 and N-S 2 would share the MP for second and third places, giving them 5 MP each instead of the present 4 MP and 8 MP. This one little slip could well cost a pair winning the event.

There's one other thing you will be expected to do on the first round of a Pairs Tournament, and that is fill in a 'curtain card' showing the hand you hold. It won't happen after the first round, as all the other first-round players will have been filling in the curtain cards for the boards they started with. It may sound like a lot of hard work, but it will all run off like water off a duck's back after you've played two or three times. The curtain cards, anyway, are for your protection. When you receive a board from another table you can check that you have the right cards and, if you haven't, get your hand corrected by the Director before you start play.

| Board No: 7 | |
SOUTH	
♠	7 4
♡	A Q J 9 8
♢	K Q 10 6
♣	A 6

That's quite enough to start you on the road to Duplicate. You would be well advised to read over the lesson before your first outing, but don't worry too much, as you'll find a little practice makes everything perfectly clear. Also don't worry if things don't seem to be working exactly as we've explained, because there are many other movements as well as the simple 'Mitchell' we have explained here. Just follow the Director's instructions and make sure you're at the right table (if you are a moving pair!), that you've got the right opponents, the right boards, and the right cards.

So now good luck to you. Face the fact that you've got a lot more to learn. This will come from further lessons, from reading, and mainly from practice. May you have as much pleasure out of your bridge, whether Rubber, Duplicate or both, as we have done.

TABLE OF STANDARD LEADS

Holding	Against Trump Contracts	Against No Trump Contracts	Holding	Against Trump Contracts	Against No Trump Contracts
'Blind' leads — i.e., when partner has not bid a suit:					
A-K-J or more	A	A	J 10 9 x x	J	J
A K Q x x x	A	A	10 9 8	10	10
A K Q x x	A	K	J 10 x x	x	x
A K Q x	A	K	A Q J x x	A*	Q
A K x	A	K	A Q 10 9 x	A	10
A K	K	K	A Q x x x	A	x
A K J 10	A	A	A J 10 x x	A	J
A K J x	A	K	A 10 9 x x	A	10
A K J x x	A	K	K J 10 x x	J	J
A K J x x x x	A	A	K 10 9 x x	10	10
A K x x x x	A	x	Q 10 9 x x	10	10
A K 10 9 x	A	10	A x x	A	x
A K x x x	A	x	K J x	x	x
K Q J x x	K	K	K x x	x	x
K Q 10 x x	K	K	Q 10 x	x	x
K Q x x x	K	x	J x x	x	x
Q J 10 x x	Q	Q	K x x x	x	x
Q J 9 x x	Q	Q	x x x	Top followed by middle**	
Q J x x x	x	x	x x	Top first	

* From this point onwards, 'blind' leads from these combinations and other like them are to be avoided if defending a suit contract, unless nothing more promising can be found.

** A more modern method is a M.U.D. lead, *M*iddle, *U*p, and *D*own, which avoids any possible confusion with a lead from a doubleton, and the loss of 'tempo' for the defence in trying to give partner a ruff on the third round.

When partner has bid during the auction and you intend to lead his bid suit, at a suit contract, always lead the ace if held. Otherwise, from three or four to an honour lead *low*. From any four cards, lead low. From a doubleton, even a doubleton honour, lead the top first. The only difference when leading against a No Trump contract, is that you should lead low from either A-x-x or A-x-x-x.

TABLE OF SCORES — RUBBER BRIDGE

Points scored below the line by declarer and partner for contracts bid and made:

For each trick over 6 bid and made

if trumps are:	♣	♦	♥	♠
Undoubled	20	20	30	30
Doubled	40	40	60	60
Redoubled	80	80	120	120

At No Trumps:

		Dbld.	Redbld.
For the first trick over six			
bid and made	40	80	160
For each subsequent trick bid			
and made	30	60	120

'Insult' bonus for making a

Doubled or redoubled contract 50 points in any contract

The first pair to win 100 points below the line, in one or more deals, scores a game. The first pair to win two games wins the Rubber.

Bonus Scores to declarer and his partner (scored *above* the line)

Little slam (12 tricks bid and made) 500 not vul., 750 vul.

Grand slam (13 tricks bid and made) 1000 not vul., 1500 vul.

Overtricks (tricks won over the number required for contract)

Undoubled .... Trick value as above

Doubled .... 100 not vul., 200 vul.

Redoubled .... 200 not vul., 400 vul.

Rubber, Game, or Part-Score:

For winning two-game Rubber .... 700 points

For winning three-game Rubber .... 500 points

Unfinished Rubber, one game .... 300 points

Unfinished Rubber, part-score only .... 50 points

Penalties: Scored above the line by defenders if contract is defeated:

	Not vul.			Vul.		
	Undbld.	Dbld.	Redbld.	Undbld.	Dbld.	Rdbld.
For first undertrick	50	100	200	100	200	400
For each subsequent undertrick	50	200	400	100	300	600

Honours:

Five trump honours in any one hand 150 points

Any four trump honours in one hand 100 points

Four aces in one hand at No Trumps 150 points

Hints for Bridge Tutors

If you are an English Bridge Union registered diploma-holding teacher you will have gone through the mill, if not of a training course, at least of a stiffish examination, both written and oral, so should have little need for these notes. But from the questions we get asked even by the qualified members of the English Bridge Union Teachers' Association, as well as many who teach without qualifications on the subject, we hope to help.

Please, registered teachers, don't take offence if some of the advice seems too elementary to use space on. A lot of it is for those who have just wandered into teaching and have no clear idea of how it should be done.

In the first place, never, *never* amble into a class of eager students, talk for a while, perhaps making notes on a blackboard, and then just deal out hands, or let the students deal them and then offer comments and advice. We know that no E.B.U. diploma-holder would do this, and many non-diploma-holders are, of course, excellent teachers too but to the others may we say please prepare your lessons, taking each subject in small doses, and then, after at most 35 minutes of explanation of the subject for the day, *give them set hands to play based on what you have just taught.*

Two words of advice here. First, having taken the trouble to work out your prepared hands and set them up before the class, write them down so that, if you take a new beginners' class next year, you won't have to do all this work again. Secondly, although each lesson should advance a step or so, always recap briefly on what you taught the previous week and, in your set hands, go back from time to time on subjects the students should (but probably won't) remember. For example, if you have taught them simple No Trump bidding and responses, and given them boards on this, and the following week you teach them 'Stayman', slip in hands from the previous week which are not suitable for 'Stayman' or they'll get the idea that they always have to bid 2 ♣ facing a 1 NT opening bid. In the same way, if you've taught Strong Twos and later taught 2 ♣ openings, in the lesson on Strong Twos slip in a hand or so which is not good enough for a Strong Two, and in the lesson on 2 ♣ bids, mix in one-bids *and* Strong Twos, so that they can't just guess that every hand should be opened with a particular bid.

Here are one or two notes for tutors who may use this book as the foundation for their course. Firstly, at the head of each 'lesson' you will find a brief summary of the contents of the lesson. This may save you hours of work when preparing your lesson, though you would be well advised to read what we have said in case your own ideas differ slightly from ours. One teacher, for example, had wrongly told her class to count points before embarking on a Strong Two opening, and was struck a trifle dumb by a student who had been to one of our courses and who firmly told her, 'That's not what the Lederers say!'

It's a hint you may well omit if you like, but we have found it a great help to extract Lesson 1 into a 2-page summary and get this sent out to all new beginners ten days or so before the start of the course. Most Adult Education Authorities are perfectly willing to do the duplicating and posting for their tutors, and it is a great asset if they have been instructed to learn the preliminaries so that, at the first lesson, you can take only quite a short time to recap. They can then be allowed to make an early start on what is really all they want to do — get the cards in their hands.

You will see in the Tutors' Notes at the head of Lesson 2 that we advise simple boards with directed contract on the play of the hand in No Trumps. The idea here, of course, is to get them quickly onto handling cards and winning tricks without burdening them too much with learning about the auction as well as the play. If you take our advice about the preliminaries, you may well be able to get onto set boards in your very first lesson — we always make sure we do. Be careful that the boards are all on the simple basic techniques of playing a hand in No Trumps, put in a slip (the back of an old curtain card will do) saying just what declarer is to play the hand in and then, for their next lesson when you have been teaching the elementary No Trump bidding set out in Lesson 3, take the same boards minus the directed contracts. We give you our solemn word that not one student will recognise them.

Another very important hint is to start each lesson by putting up the heading of what you are going to teach on the blackboard. It may sound a silly thing, but more than half the students will probably be wives with husbands who think they play good bridge at home. The first question husband will ask when wife gets home is 'What did you learn to-day?', and a good solid answer such as 'Weak No Trump Opening Bids and Responses' may well lead to a happy hour or so of question and answer. We can assure you this is true, because of the number of wives who will come back the following week and say, 'My husband says he'd never do so and so . . .' and then you can explain your point even more fully — and sometimes even get a convert from the home!

It won't really matter which order you take the lessons in. If you are a strong No Trump addict you will want to teach that before you teach the weak No Trump, for example. Also you will run into particular classes which clamour for a lesson on some specific subject such as opening leads or covering honours. All right — give them that lesson by all means, but make sure its content doesn't run too far ahead of what they have learned already.

Another all-important point is not to allow beginners to come up against difficult situations they haven't yet learned to handle. Bad trump breaks and failing finesses will make them lose confidence — give them straightforward momma-poppa hands on which all their contracts succeed, if they play them correctly, as though they were in Disneyland. They'll find out soon enough for themselves what can so often happen when they get out into the big wide world! Of course, if you are a good enough teacher to enthuse them to keep on into a second, or even a third year, you will be taking them into these higher flights, but until then shelter them and, above all, let them see what fun Contract Bridge can be.

On a different note, never ask individual students questions they can't answer. It makes them feel fools and you'll find they stop attending your classes. Always encourage them to ask questions, emphasising that when learning bridge, no question is a silly question. You'll probably find that if one student asks a question about something she hasn't understood, half the rest of the class hasn't really understood it either.

Finally, to return for a moment to what we said earlier about using prepared hands set with the subject matter of what you have just taught. Two points are of importance here. For the most part teach them to bid up — not to miss their games or slams — but from time to time introduce rubber bridge hands to emphasise part-score bidding. The other point is the importance of using, for the main, set hands. If you don't you'll create complete chaos because practically every hand will contain something way beyond their ken such as a run of 2 ♣ openers when they've only learned about one-bids!

Index